The British Association for Shooting & Conservation

HANDBOOK OF SHOOTING
THE SPORTING SHOTGUN

The following Open Seasons will apply

SPECIES	OPEN SEASON
Red Grouse	1 September, 1987 to 30 September, 1987
Mallard, Teal, Gadwall, Wigeon, Pintail, Shoveler, Scaup, Tufted Duck, Pochard, Goldeneye, Golden Plover, Snipe, Jack Snipe.	1 September, 1987 to 31 January, 1988
Grey and Red Legged Partridge	1 November, 1987 to 15 November, 1987
Cock Pheasant, Woodcock, Curlew	1 November, 1987 to 31 January, 1988
All deer species (but excluding red deer in Co. Kerry) Males	1 September, 1987 to 28 February, 1988
Females	1 November, 1987 to 31 January, 1988
Hares (excluding the following townlands in Co. Wexford: North East Slob, North West Slob, Big Island, Beggerin Island and the Raven)	26 September 1987 to 28 February, 1988
Woodpigeon	1st June, 1987 to 31 January, 1988

87/88

WILDLIFE SERVICE
LEESON LANE
DUBLIN 2

The British Association for Shooting & Conservation

HANDBOOK OF SHOOTING
THE SPORTING SHOTGUN

Edited by
G. D. Turner

PELHAM BOOKS

First published in Great Britain by
Pelham Books Ltd
44 Bedford Square
London WC1B 3DU
1983

British Library Cataloguing in Publication Data

Handbook of shooting.
  I. Hunting – Great Britain
  I. Turner, G. D.
    799.2113'-0941   SK185
ISBN 0 7207 1416 8 (hardback)
ISBN 0 7207 1434 6 (paperback)

Typeset by Rowland Phototypesetting
Bury St Edmunds Suffolk
Printed & bound in Great Britain by
Blantyre Printing & Binding Co Ltd
Glasgow

ILLUSTRATIONS

Full colour illustrations of quarry species and black
and white line drawings, unless otherwise acknowledged, by John Paley; photographs by Adrian Horgan;
drawings of gundogs in Chapter 10 by Ann Seward;
distribution maps and shooting-season drawings in
Chapter 6 by Ian Hepburn.

ACKNOWLEDGEMENTS

The British Association for Shooting and Conservation gratefully acknowledges the following:
Clay Pigeon Shooting Association (C.P.S.A.) for their
kind permission to reproduce notes on how to shoot a
moving target in Appendix 5; the British Proof Authorities for permission to reproduce British proof marks
and the Spanish Proof Authorities for permission to
reproduce Spanish proof marks in Appendix 3; Her
Majesty's Stationery Office for permission to reproduce an application form for a shotgun certificate and a
specimen shotgun certificate; Ian Hepburn for technical advice and contribution to the quarry identification section; and the following members of the
B.A.S.C. staff who have all contributed knowledge and
expertise: Denis Graham-Hogg, Information Officer;
John Harradine B.Sc., PhD., Research Co-Ordinator;
Tony Laws B.Sc. (Tech), Conservation Officer; David
Leathart, Assistant Development Officer; John
Richards B.A., N.D.A., M.R.A.C., Director – De-
velopment; John Swift M.A., M.Phil., M.B.O.U.,
Director – Conservation and Research; Gerry Turner
B.A., Cert.Ed.M.I.T.D., Development Education
Officer.

Contents

Foreword

by HRH The Prince Philip, Duke of Edinburgh

Patron of the British Association for Shooting and Conservation

To the uninitiated almost every leisure occupation appears to be rather simple, if not childish. Oscar Wilde's comment about foxhunting that it was a case of the 'unspeakable in full pursuit of the uneatable' reflects this deep-rooted suspicion of anything strange or partly understood.

There is obviously much more to these occupations than is apparent at first sight. The fisherman may look as if he is just dangling a hook in the water, but anyone with experience knows that this appearance is deceptive. Golf may look as if it is just a matter of hitting a little white ball about the country and walking after it, but the volume of media coverage of golf tournaments and the shelves of books on the game suggest that its challenge fascinates a great many people.

Shooting is no exception. In fact, as this book makes clear, in order to enjoy it and to practise it sensibly and safely, needs a great deal of knowledge and skill in a number of different departments.

The first rule of sporting shooting is that it must always follow the principles of good husbandry.

Farmers don't eat their seed corn and cattlemen see that they maintain their stock of breeding cows: likewise, responsible shooting people always remember that there will be another season next year.

The second rule is that shooting practised thoughtlessly and irresponsibly is almost bound to result in cruelty. The intention must always be to kill cleanly and inflict the least possible suffering on the quarry. Therefore the chapters on Behaviour in the Field and Codes of Practice are extremely important.

How to achieve these ends, and a great deal more extremely useful guidance and information, has been collected together in this book which I am quite sure will be of the greatest value to young and old, beginners or old hands alike.

The British Association for Shooting and Conservation

Stanley Duncan, a Humber estuary wildfowler, founded the Association in 1908 in response to the growing threats to wildfowl and their habitat. From its inception until the 1950s the Wild-fowlers' Association of Great Britain and Ireland (WAGBI) remained a modest but genuinely successful and respected body.

But growth was essential if sporting shooting was to be adequately protected. Recognising that strength is in numbers, the concerted effort to recruit membership resulted in the title being changed, first to WAGBI – for Wildfowling and Rough-shooting, and later to WAGBI – for Shooting and Conservation. Additional strength was provided when the Gamekeepers' Association of the United Kingdom, itself founded in 1900, amalgamated with WAGBI.

Membership support continued to grow but many thousands of people interested in shooting still could not identify with the Association. So it was that, in 1981, the Association changed its title to The BRITISH ASSOCIATION for SHOOTING and CONSERVATION in order fully to represent sporting shooting. Details of membership benefits and advantages may be obtained by writing to the B.A.S.C., Marford Mill, Rossett, Wrexham, Clwyd, LL12 oHL.

Proficiency Award Scheme

WHY HAS THE PROFICIENCY AWARD SCHEME BEEN INTRODUCED?

Traditionally, the Association has placed a great deal of emphasis on education and training. Some time ago the Education Sub-Committee produced a set of Codes of Practice for the sport to guide those seeking basic information. This course of action was undertaken because we believe that as an Association we have a duty to encourage high standards of safety, sportsmanship and courtesy among those who enjoy the legitimate sport of shooting. Following the Codes of Practice series we are now implementing a Proficiency Award Scheme on a purely voluntary basis which has been set up to offer members a way of improving their knowledge.

The primary purpose of this Handbook for sporting shotgun shooting is to teach shotgun safety, sportsmanship and courtesy. There are also other objectives, such as to teach country lores and traditions, the law relating to shooting and generally to enable those who take part in the sport to derive far greater enjoyment in the knowledge that they are conducting themselves according to acceptable standards of behaviour in the shooting field.

Much of the criticism which is levelled against shooting sports is as a direct result of either misunderstanding or of bad behaviour witnessed in the field. The rights and privileges of sportsmen to continue to enjoy their sport and the satisfaction of conserving the countryside and wildlife depends very much on the behaviour of all sportsmen. They will be judged by their attitude and behaviour.

The social structure of the shooting community has altered considerably in the last few years and there are many now who wish to take up the sport, or indeed who have entered it, but have no real knowledge of shooting, of the lores and traditions of the countryside, or of the quarry species they pursue and of the management needs of those species.

The Proficiency Award Scheme has therefore been introduced to give everyone who shoots a practical means of attaining the B.A.S.C. Ideal – 'That all who shoot lawfully in Britain conduct themselves according to the highest standards of safety, sportsmanship and courtesy, with full respect for their quarry and a practical interest in wildlife conservation and the wellbeing of the countryside.'

HOW TO ENTER FOR THE PROFICIENCY AWARD

The Award will be offered upon the satisfactory completion of two assessments, one theoretical and one practical, which will be conducted at a number of Regional Proficiency Award Scheme Centres. Those wishing to apply may prepare for the assessment simply by reading this Handbook or, alternatively, they can attend a Proficiency Award Scheme Course at a number of Regional Centres. The course of instruction is given on one evening a week for ten weeks.

To apply to qualify for the Award or take the course of instruction leading to the theoretical and practical assessment, write to the Development Division, B.A.S.C. Headquarters, Marford Mill, Rossett, Clwyd, LL12 0HL. Once your application has been received you will be informed of both the assessment and course details. Satisfactory completion of both the theoretical and practical assessments will be acknowledged by the presentation of a certificate and a badge. Many B.A.S.C. affiliated clubs are proposing to use the Proficiency Award Scheme as a method of vetting potential new club members.

WHO CAN QUALIFY FOR THE AWARD?

The Award Scheme is open to all members of the British Association for Shooting and Conservation over the age of fourteen. Whilst we recognise that newcomers to the sport will benefit the most, experienced sportsmen wishing to broaden their knowledge will also be welcome.

G. D. TURNER
Development Education Officer

MEASUREMENTS

Wherever possible, both metric and imperial measurements have been given. But the imperial unit only has been used in some instances, for example, when quoting from statutes.

Man has sought game and wildfowl for centuries, initially for food and latterly for recreation. When man is hungry, to kill the quarry is the over-riding objective, but when his larder is adequately supplied the natural impulse to hunt and pursue his quarry remains. The hunter has become a sportsman and his sport has evolved clearly defined patterns of behaviour which make up the sporting ethic.

It is a fundamental aspect of sportsmanship that the pursuit of the quarry be undertaken with safety, courtesy, respect for the quarry and the countryside, and without endangering other people. The sportsman's conduct will then be beyond reproach.

Shooting cannot take place without affecting the countryside as a whole and people who shoot should be aware of the implications of their own actions and also of other pressures. Afforestation, modern farming techniques, increasing leisure time and improved means of travel from urban areas into the countryside have all brought increasing pressures on the countryside and wildlife.

In consequence, it has become necessary to strengthen the sporting ethic by developing well defined codes of practice and statutory regulations for shooting sports. Knowledge and a practical application of these are a prerequisite of sportsmanship. Those who shoot without this basic knowledge are likely not only to endanger themselves and their fellow men, but will also bring a great deal of discredit to the sport and pose yet another threat to its future.

THE NEED FOR CONSERVATION

So many factors affect wildlife in our environment today that the interdependence of all of man's activities must be taken into account. The sportsman must become involved in the broader issues concerning wildlife conservation and the management of the countryside.

As will be seen, wildlife is dependent on healthy habitats, but these are being damaged or destroyed at an alarming rate. Thirty thousand acres (over 12,000 hectares) of countryside are destroyed annually by urban development; 4 per cent of the country's most valuable wildlife areas are damaged each year. Hedges are being uprooted, woodlands felled and wetlands drained. Pollution in various forms further disrupts the balance of nature.

CONSERVATION CONCEPTS

Wildlife and game conservation involves the protection, management and wise use of plants, animals and their environment.

HABITAT

Habitat is the environment that supplies everything wildlife needs to sustain healthy populations. Different wildlife species require particular habitats. Habitats are of broadly distinctive types and tend to be classified according to their location, flora and fauna, physical characteristics and geology; for example, a lowground deciduous woodland area. Each habitat type provides the food, cover, water and space for the species living there.

HABITAT MANAGEMENT

Habitats can be managed for different purposes; not only for nature conservation, but also for game production and recreation. The availability of food, cover, water and open space is managed to achieve the desired purpose. Countryside which provides a mixture of habitats is clearly desirable since it is able to support more bird and animal species.

It is also important to bear in mind that each wildlife species occupies an unique 'niche' in the environment; if its particular habitat changes in character or is altered by management, some species may do well and others decline. Excessive management of, for example, a woodland habitat for Pheasants, or a pond for Mallard, can sometimes harm other wildlife species.

CARRYING CAPACITY

It follows that a given habitat will support a certain number of individuals of a particular species. This number is called the 'carrying capacity'. When numbers exceed the habitat's carrying capacity the excess animals fail to breed because there is, for example, insufficient nesting cover, or they may die from starvation.

Since a habitat has a fixed carrying capacity it is possible for man to crop the excess without affecting the well-being of particular species. Indeed it may help preserve the balance between species essential for the preservation of habitat.

POPULATION DYNAMICS

In conservation it is important to understand why populations increase or decline. This is the biological science of 'population dynamics'. A population of animals is a group of animals that occupies a particular area. Whether the population increases in numbers or declines depends upon the balance between the birth and death rates over the years, allied to any immigration or emigration of individuals that may take place, into or out of that area.

Most animal populations have an enormous capacity for increase, but as we have seen the increase levels off very quickly if they run short of some essential life requirement. Other factors, such as severe weather, may temporarily reduce the population but it will soon recover, if all other factors remain constant.

THE ANNUAL CYCLE

It is important for the conservationist to understand what goes on throughout the whole year.

In spring, adults produce young which take advantage of the plentiful food available in summer. Populations are then at their highest and may greatly exceed the carrying capacity of the habitat. The subsequent mortality of young is usually heavy in order to restore the balance of numbers, but many or all of the remaining population will move to winter quarters where most of them will be able to find the necessary food and shelter, although some species tend to stay in the same area throughout the year. Some animals may find food in short supply during the winter and may die as a result. In other species the excess will die in spring on return to the breeding areas.

MIGRATION

The regular annual movement between breeding and wintering grounds is called migration. Some species migrate many thousands of miles.

A large proportion of the ducks, geese, Woodcock and Snipe which winter in Britain breed in the Baltic countries, the Soviet Union and Iceland. In certain species, for example Mallard, some individuals migrate long distances while others remain in Britain all the year. Such species are called partial migrants.

PREDATION

Those wildlife species that live by preying on others are called predators. Whilst the predator's effect on prey populations is normally part of the natural balance of nature, there are circumstances, as will be seen later, when the consequences are severe and the predators need to be controlled.

PRACTICAL CONSERVATION

The shooting man is only part of the overall countryside conservation picture. Careful planning and cooperation between different groups of countryside users is important if everyone is to play a positive and constructive part.

The key to conservation is habitat and there are two themes to a habitat conservation strategy. Firstly, the protection of the special areas classified as being of national and regional importance; secondly, the maintenance and management of local habitats on the shoot or farm.

SPECIAL AREAS

Some habitats are valuable because they are part of an attractive landscape. Others hold very rare plants or animals or are good examples of characteristic types of habitat. Such areas of landscape or conservation value may be given official designations which render them subject to planning controls or afford them protection and management. (The categories of special areas are listed and defined in Appendix 1.)

Many of these areas of nature conservation interest are under the management influence of sportsmen and should be managed very much with this special interest in mind. Numerous examples exist of joint management schemes between sporting and nature conservation groups (e.g. sportsmen assist in wardening and practical habitat work while shooting under an agreed programme). It is one of the sporting community's top priorities to

13

participate in the protection and management of these sites.

HABITAT CONSERVATION
ON THE SHOOT AND
FARM
Local habitat conservation involves various forms of site management. Management for duck, for example, may include the creation of ponds, the management of wetlands, and the regulation of recreational activities, including shooting.

GAME MANAGEMENT
Shooting men should make every effort to promote the wild breeding populations of Pheasants, partridges, grouse and other non-migratory quarry. This can be achieved in part by the creation and preservation of habitat (for example, by the planting of suitable small woodlands, preserving hedgerows, fencing off the unused corners of fields and the growing of game crops), the controlled use of agricultural chemicals and sympathetic farming practices. All these measures assist not only game species, but many forms of wildlife.

In addition, Pheasants and partridges may be hand-reared and released to boost the wild populations.

In the upland areas of moorland, grouse management involves very much the same principles, but the application is slightly different. Instead of planting and clearing, heather burning does essentially the same job. A patchwork effect is created by burning and this encourages young heather growth, on which the grouse feed, whilst at the same time leaving older heather to provide nesting cover and protection from predators.

STOCKING
Artificial stocking can be useful to reintroduce a species to an area where it no longer occurs naturally, or where a population is very scarce, but it needs to be done in the full knowledge of the biological implications. Detailed consultation should invariably be undertaken before reintroduction programmes are initiated.

Stocking is, of course, a traditional activity in relation to certain quarry species, particularly Pheasants, Mallard and partridges, as will be seen later. But there is no point in introducing birds into a habitat which is incapable of supporting them. For success, stocking has to be carried on in conjunction with the proper management of the habitat in order to provide sufficient food and cover for the extra birds which the habitat has to support.

INTRODUCTION OF
NON-NATIVE SPECIES
The introduction of non-native species to a habitat is an undesirable aspect of stocking which is controlled by law. Most aliens find their habitats unsuitable and disappear soon after release, although some may become established. There are, however, serious dangers in introducing alien species into a new habitat. Introduced species or escapees create problems because there are insufficient natural enemies to control their numbers in their new environment; for example, the Grey Squirrel and, more recently, Mink in Britain.

RESEARCH

Detailed knowledge of wildlife populations and their habitats is important for effective conservation. A part of the sportsman's effort should therefore be devoted to gathering and maintaining up-to-date information on shooting activity and quarry population levels.

Thus every would-be sportsman is encouraged to start and maintain a game book for every shooting occasion.

Whilst such a game book will be kept primarily for personal reasons, the sportsman is in an unique position to contribute information on shooting and on various aspects of wildfowl and game biology. In this way, he can assist his Association to establish a scientific base for the future of the sport and to integrate shooting with the requirements of wildlife conservation.

Details of a number of surveys conducted by the British Association for Shooting and Conservation are listed in Appendix 2.

THE FUTURE OF WILDLIFE

The way that the sportsman behaves and acts will be contributory to deciding whether wildlife has a future or not. For this reason it is extremely important that every would-be sportsman is aware of the implications and of how he can contribute.

SHOOTING

The future of wildlife may depend to a significant degree on land management interests having a reason for conserving habitats. On account of their limited resources the conservation organisations must concentrate on conserving the most valuable wildlife areas comprising a very small percentage of the total rural landscape area. Other interests and land uses, in particular shooting, are extremely important in managing and conserving both these and the rest of our countryside.

2   Shotguns and Cartridges

The shooter's choice of shotgun will largely be determined by the kind of quarry to be sought and the likely range at which it will most often be encountered.

SHOTGUNS

DEFINITION OF A SHOTGUN

The Firearms Act 1968 defines a shotgun as being a smooth-bore gun with a barrel not less than 24 inches in length and not being an air gun. (Part 1 Section 1)
This definition requires further explanation as it allows for a number of variations incorporating a number of different features.

THE COMPONENT PARTS OF A SHOTGUN

There are various types and styles of shotguns available. The 'standard game gun' is here examined, since it is the type most commonly used.

The standard game gun

The standard game gun is a double-barrel side-by-side hammerless ejector 12-bore shotgun of drop-down opening style. It has a top lever and barrels between 63.5cm (25in) and 76cm (30in) in length, with either a side or boxlock action, double triggers and an automatic safety catch. It has fairly open choke and is chambered for 6.4cm (2½in) or 7cm (2¾in) cartridges. It has a stock, fore-end and rib.

Standard game gun

Standard game gun showing:
1 double barrels   6 double triggers
2 side-by-side   7 safety catch
3 hammerless   8 stock
4 top lever   9 fore-end
5 boxlock   10 rib

You must be able to identify the following components and features of a shotgun:

Double barrel and side-by-side

Double barrel means that the shotgun has two barrels; side-by-side refers to the positioning of those two barrels.

position of barrels: side-by-side

Over-and-under

Alternatively, the two barrels may be placed one above the other. This style of shotgun is known as an 'over-and-under'.

position of barrels: 'over-and-under'

Single and three-barrelled shotguns

The most common alternative to the double-barrel shotgun is the single barrel. Guns have been made which have three barrels, the third usually being placed centrally below the other two in a side-by-side position. In such guns the third barrel is normally rifled (i.e. grooved) and is intended for use against large ground game. These guns are more common on the continent than in the United Kingdom. You cannot possess such a gun in the United Kingdom unless you have a Firearms Certificate on which the gun is specified.

The construction of shotgun barrels

Modern shotgun barrels are made of steel and are either drilled or drawn out of a solid cylindrical piece of steel.

Damascus barrels

iron

steel

An alternative method of constructing shotgun barrels by twisting thin strands of iron and steel together and welding them into a barrel shape is now obsolete. Barrels made in this manner are known as Damascus barrels; they may be found on a number of guns still in use. Many will not have been proved (see p. 31) for modern nitro powders.

composition of Damascus barrels: the iron and steel strands when welded together will be formed into a barrel shape

Hammerless

Hammerless refers to the absence of visible exterior hammers.

Hammerless guns were first patented around 1860. Hammer guns are still in common use, but a number of older ones may not have been proved (see p. 31) for use with modern cartridges.

hammerless gun

hammer gun

Ejector

The ejector throws out, or ejects, fired cartridges when the gun is opened; non-fired cartridges are not ejected.

The alternative to the ejector is known as the non-ejector. Non-ejectors do not throw out fired cartridges, but will lift empty cases slightly – thus enabling the user to grip the cartridge and manually extract it.

Semi-automatic (see p. 25) and pump-action shotguns (see p. 25) eject as part of the sequence of firing and bringing up the next cartridge into the chamber.

Bore of a shotgun

Shotguns are classified by the size of the bore. The bore is measured by the number of perfectly spherical balls of pure lead, each exactly fitting the interior diameter of the barrel, required to make up 1lb in weight.

how a bore is measured: 12-bore

Therefore, because a 20-bore requires 20 such lead spheres, and a 12-bore requires 12, the 20-bore must be of a smaller bore than the 12-bore.

The different bores available are 4, 8, 10, 12, 16, 20 and 28 bore. There is also a .410. The .410 is not measured by the number of spherical lead balls, each exactly fitting the diameter of the barrel, required to make up 1lb in weight, but refers to the actual diameter of the barrel as four-tenths of an inch.

The standard game gun is a 12-bore. The 12-bore is suitable for all types of sporting shotgun shooting provided the appropriate cartridge is used (see p. 26).

The 4, 8 and 10-bore are normally used only for coastal wildfowling, although the 12-bore is perfectly adequate. The 4, 8 and 10-bore are no longer in common use.

The 16-bore is suitable for most forms of inland shooting, but is more commonly used on the Continent than in this country.

The 20-bore is a suitable light-weight game and general purpose inland gun.

The 28-bore and the .410 are normally used to introduce youngsters to shotguns, but their limited range severely limits their value and could discourage youngsters from continuing in the sport. It may be advisable to wait until the beginner is capable of handling a 20 or 16-bore.

Drop-down action refers to the manner in which the shotgun is opened for the purposes of loading and reloading.

Not all shotguns have a drop-down action. On semi-automatic and pump-action shotguns the barrels do not drop down to enable the user to insert a cartridge into the chamber; instead, the cartridge is placed in the chamber as part of the manual or semi-automatic process of firing. On bolt-action shotguns the cartridge is inserted into the chamber which is exposed by pulling the bolt back.

semi-automatic action
(shown open)

bolt-action shotgun

Advantage of the drop-down action

A distinct advantage of the drop-down style is that it allows the user to easily check that the barrels are clear of an obstruction before loading, or after an obstruction may have entered the muzzle (for example, when shooting in snow or mud, and after any abnormal noise or recoil on firing).

Top lever

The top lever is the manual means by which the standard game gun is opened.

Although the top lever is standard, some guns have an under lever; some have side levers, but these are rare.

Non drop-down guns do not require opening levers.

side lever

Boxlock and sidelock action

Boxlock and sidelock are the alternative actions to be found in standard game guns. The action is, in simplified terms, the firing mechanism.

Boxlocks are cheaper to manufacture than sidelocks because they are simpler in design and have fewer components.

Sidelock actions are larger and heavier than boxlock actions, but allow for easier access to the mechanism for cleaning.

Triggers

The majority of double-barrel shotguns are fitted with double triggers, one for each barrel.

On a side-by-side with double triggers, the right hand side-trigger fires the right barrel and the left-hand side-trigger fires the left barrel. The right trigger is in front of the left trigger. (This applies to a right-hand gun, which is the manner in which most are manufactured. Left-hand guns are normally only made to specification.)

Double-barrel shotguns can be fitted with a single trigger which may or may not be selective. If the single trigger is selective, the shooter can choose which barrel he fires first, thus allowing for a choice of choke. The selecting device is normally incorporated into the safety catch. The single non-selective trigger will fire the right barrel first and the left barrel second.

On an over-and-under shotgun with double triggers, the right trigger fires the bottom barrel and the left trigger fires the top barrel.

The Safety Catch

The safety catch bolts the triggers so that they cannot be pulled. This does not mean, however, that the internal hammers are locked: they remain cocked and poised over the cartridges. The gun could be discharged by a knock or a jar, or even a hard pull on the trigger.

A shotgun with cartridges in the chambers is not safe – no matter what position the safety catch is in.

Automatic safety catches

Safety catches may be: automatic, i.e. returning to safe when the gun is opened.

Non-automatic safety catches

Or: non-automatic, i.e. not returning as part of the process of opening the gun.

Take extra care with safety catches which are non-automatic.

Do not rely on any safety catch to make a shotgun safe

Many semi-automatic pump-action shotguns have a sliding-button safety catch on the side of the action which is usually non-automatic.

See p. 38 for recommendation on the use of the safety catch.

Choke

Choke refers to constriction at the muzzle end of the bore of a shotgun: that is at the end of the barrel which gives a certain amount of inward propulsion to the shot. This is necessary because as soon as the pellets leave the muzzle they begin to spread; the further they travel, the more they spread. Eventually they will spread so much that not enough pellets will hit the target.

Degrees of choke

a degree of choke
at the muzzle

The five degrees of choke are:
  (i) Full choke – tightest degree of restriction
  (ii) Three-quarter choke
  (iii) Half choke
  (iv) Quarter choke
  (v) One-eighth choke (often referred to as improved cylinder).

True cylinder

Finally, if there is no degree of restriction at the muzzle and the diameter is the same at the muzzle as along the whole bore this is known as true cylinder.

Effect of choke

Pattern is the distribution of pellets in a given circle at a given range; the tightest pattern, i.e. the greatest number of pellets in that circle, is produced by full choke and the most open by the true cylinder.

pattern produced by true cylinder (*top*)
and full choke (*bottom*)

A standard load 12-bore cartridge will place the following number of pellets in a 76cm (30in) circle at a range of 35m (about 40yd):

Degree of Choke	Percentage of Pellets ex 300		
Full	225		75%
Three-quarter	195		65%
Half	180	in a 76cm (30in) circle	60%
Quarter	150	at 35m (about 40yd)	50%
Improved cylinder	135		45%
True cylinder	120		40%

From the foregoing it might be assumed that the degree of choke which places the greatest number of pellets onto the target is the most desirable and that full choke would be most suitable. This would be true if all shots fired were accurately aimed and if all shots were taken at 35m (about 40yd) range. In Britain most shooting is at targets much less than 35m (about 40yd) away. Few trees exceed 14m (15yd) in height and most inland shooting occurs at about tree-top height.

The degree of choke used is largely dependant upon personal choice; but many, if not most, people use more open than tight chokes, often with improved cylinder in the right barrel and quarter or half choke in the left.

Removal of choke	**Choke can be removed, but it cannot be replaced**. The only exception is recess choke where it can be replaced to a certain extent. Most guns are fitted with normal and not recess choke.
Recess choke	Recess choke is usually found only in top-class shotguns. On a standard side-by-side game gun the right barrel has a more open choke than the left. On over-and-under shotguns the lower barrel usually has a more open choke than the top barrel. Single-barrel shotguns are limited to one choke (unless fitted with one of the proprietary brands of variable choke devices which are now available).
Tight choke	**A tight choke does not increase the range of a shotgun (see p. 27).**
Chambers	The chamber of a shotgun is that part of the barrel nearest to the action into which the cartridge is inserted. Most 12-bore shotguns are chambered for 65mm (2½in) or 70mm (2¾in) cartridges. **It is dangerous to fire a 70mm (2¾in) cartridge in a gun chambered for 65mm (2½in) cartridges.**
Stock	The stock has two functions: one is to house the action; the other is to ensure that the shotgun when brought up to the shoulder is correctly aligned with the shooter's 'master' eye.
Master eye	Everybody has a master eye: the 'master' eye looks directly at objects. It is essential that you shoot from the same shoulder as your master eye. If you have a right master eye, shoot from the right shoulder and if you have a left master eye, shoot from the left shoulder. To determine which is your 'master' eye follow this simple procedure: 1 Hold a pencil upright at arm's length in your left hand. 2 Look through both eyes and line the pencil point up with an object on the other side of the room (for example, a light switch). 3 Place your right hand over your right eye. If the pencil and the object are no longer in line, you have a right master eye. 4 Place your right hand over your left eye. The object will still be in line with the pencil. If, when you placed your right hand over the right eye, the object and the pencil were still in line, then you have a left master eye. Shotgun stocks are traditionally made of walnut which can be bent or cast to suit the shooter's requirements.

A stock is measured as shown in the illustration below:

how a stock is measured:
A bend to comb
B bend to heel
C length to heel
D length to butt
E length to toe

'Cast' of a stock

The term 'cast' refers to the degree to which the stock is bent out of straight in relation to the line of the barrel(s) in order to bring the barrel(s) in line with the user's master eye.

Cast is measured at the butt and is termed 'cast off' if it is to the right and 'cast on' if it is to the left.

Shapes of shotgun stocks

The standard game gun usually has a 'straight' stock. This enables the user to manipulate the rear trigger. Single-trigger shotguns are normally fitted with a pistol or semi-pistol grip.

different stocks: straight (*left*) semi-pistol (*middle*) full pistol (*right*)

The fore-end

One of the functions of the fore-end is that it provides the forward grip for the shooter. It should not be too smooth and it should be large enough to prevent the fingers of the forward hand encroaching upon the rib and thus obstructing the line of sight.

Most standard game guns are fitted with a narrow fore-end, known as an English fore-end; a common variant is the broad American style beaver-tail fore-end. Choice is largely dependent upon personal preferences. The fore-end also serves to lock the barrels into position.

English fore-end

American beaver-tail fore-end

The rib	On a side-by-side shotgun the rib is used to secure the barrels to each other and as a sighting device along which to line up the barrels on to the target. On a single barrel, and over-and-under shotgun, the rib is used solely as a sighting plane.
PUMP-ACTION AND SEMI-AUTOMATIC SHOTGUNS	Pump-action and semi-automatic shotguns can be operated on one of three principles: manual, gas pressure or recoil.
Pump action:	Manually operated pump-action shotguns have a sliding fore-end which, when pulled back and pushed forward, ejects the fired cartridge and brings the next cartridge from the magazine into the chamber, ready for firing. The magazines usually have five or three cartridge capacity.
Gas operated semi-automatic shotguns	Gas pressure-operated semi-automatics work by an impulsion of the propellant gas into a cylinder which operates a mechanism in the breech which will eject the fired cartridge.
Recoil operated semi-automatic shotguns:	Recoil operated semi-automatic shotguns work by a process of barrel or chamber recoil generated by the shot. The principle remains the same as for the manually operated pump-action shotgun except that the 'pump' occurs automatically on recoil.
Side-by-side and semi-automatic shotguns	**The standard side-by-side shotgun has stood the test of time and is universally accepted whereas pump-action and semi-automatic shotguns are not always welcomed on formal driven shoots** (see Chapter 8). **This is part of the lore of sporting shotgun shooting.** **With the introduction of the Wildlife and Countryside Act 1981 the sporting use of semi-automatic shotguns has been limited as such guns are prohibited for shooting wildfowl and game birds unless they are restricted to fire not more than three cartridges in succession without re-loading.**

SHOTGUN CARTRIDGES

As with shotguns, the shotgun cartridge will be examined by discussing the standard 12-bore game cartridge and the variations available.

The standard 12-bore game cartridge is 65mm (2½in) in length, has a case which is made of plastic and which is crimp closed and throws a load of 1 1/16 oz.

composition of standard game cartridge

1 case
2 wad
3 powder
4 crimp closure
5 shot (load)
6 primer

The length of the cartridge

The standard 12-bore game cartridge is 65 mm (2½in) in length. A 65mm (2½in) cartridge is suitable for use in a 70mm (2¾in) chamber gun. Cartridges which are longer than the chamber length of the gun should not be used.

Variations range from 50mm (2in) cartridges to 80mm (3¼in) 8-bore cartridges. The cartridge is normally longer in the 8-bore as it incorporates a heavier load (see p. 27).

The cartridge case

The case is the outer shell of the cartridge. It has three functions: it is a container for the remaining components of the cartridge; it has to retain the shot until the correct moment; it has to seal the chamber so that all the pressure is directed down the barrel and is not allowed to escape.

It is preferable that the case is waterproof and for this reason cartridges are now commonly manufactured with plastic or polyethylene cases.

Cartridges were previously manufactured with paper cases; the main disadvantages with paper cases are that they are not waterproof and may warp if they become damp. Paper cases may also split if they become abnormally dry.

Store paper cases at normal room temperature, out of the sun and away from sources of heat and damp.

An advantage of paper-cased cartridges is that the case disintegrates if left on the ground. Plastic cases do not. The most sensible approach is to pick up all empty cartridge cases and not to leave litter.

Crimp closures

Crimp closure refers to the manner in which the cartridge is sealed in order to retain its components. The case is made sufficiently long to allow the top to be turned in towards the centre in a star pattern.

Roll closures

The alternative method is roll closure. The end of the cartridge is pressed over a wad which retains the components.

The Load

This refers to the weight of the lead shot. Shot is small balls of lead of various sizes. In descending order from single to dust shot, these are:

Single
L.G.
S.G.
Sp. S.G.
S.S.G.
A.A.A.
B.B.
1 2 3 4 5 6 7 8 9
Dust shot

Recommended shot sizes

The following shot sizes are normally recommended in a standard 12-bore game gun for the following species:

Partridge 6/7	Pheasant 5/6/7	Snipe 8
Grouse 6/7	Woodcock 7	Geese BB/1/3
Pigeon 6/7	Teal 6/7	Mallard 4/5/6
Hare 4/5	Rabbit 5/6	Squirrel 7

The standard game load is 30g ($1\frac{1}{16}$oz) of number 6 shot, although many game shooters will use either No 5 or No 7 shot.

The loads may range from the 57g (2oz) in the 8-bore used for wildfowling to the smaller loads used in the .410 such as the $\frac{5}{16}$oz load.

A heavier load does not increase the effective range of a shotgun.

Shotgun range

The range of a shotgun is not simply the maximum range at which a shotgun is capable of killing a particular quarry. This would mean that a shotgun or cartridge combination which was capable of killing by hitting a vital spot on the target occasionally could result in a large number of instances of wounding without killing.

In order to define the range of a shotgun we can do no better than to quote Gough Thomas from his book *Shotguns and Cartridges for Game and Clays* in which he states: '. . . the maximum effective range of a gun in relation to a given kind of game is the greatest range at which it is reasonably certain that a clean kill will be made by a truly aimed shot.'

In effect, this means that with a standard load 12-bore cartridge the maximum effective range will be 32–7m (35–40yd). In the case of geese this will be reduced to 27m (30yd).

Smaller bore guns will have a correspondingly lower maximum effective range. All bores create similar patterns, but in the smaller bore guns the effect of this will be to reduce the number of pellets in the target and therefore to reduce the maximum effective range.

THE CARE AND MAINTENANCE OF A SHOTGUN

There are three good reasons for maintaining a shotgun in good working order: (*i*) to ensure that it remains in a safe condition; (*ii*) to reduce the risk of mechanical malfunction at any time; (*iii*) to preserve an asset which will appreciate if well looked after.

There are a number of methods and materials which may be used. The following is one method which will enable a shotgun to be kept clean and rust free.

The recommended cleaning kit consists of:

a cleaning rod
tissue paper, kitchen paper or rolled-up newspaper
a proprietary brand of gun cleaner – in either oil or spray form
a phosphor bronze brush
a lambswool mop
pipe-cleaners
a soft cloth/rag

The following recommendations are based on the assumption that the shotgun has been fired on a particularly wet day.

First detach the barrels from the stock.

TO CLEAN THE STOCK

Hold the stock firmly and give it a good shake. On a wet day water which has penetrated the mechanism will thus be shaken out.

Remove all visible water from the exterior of the stock.

Remove any mud, dirt or blood from the stock and clean the chequering, possibly with a soft toothbrush, to remove any dirt.

Rub over the mechanism with an oily rag.

TO CLEAN THE FORE-END

Use the same method as for the stock.

TO CLEAN THE BARRELS

Remove all visible water from the barrels and run a piece of tissue, as tightly as possible, along the guttering beside the rib.

Fold or roll-up the newspaper or tissue and push it through the barrels with the cleaning rod – the tissue should be as tight as possible – from the chamber to the muzzle. This will remove the worst of the fouling and will enable you to keep your cleaning materials relatively clean.

The next stage is to attach the phosphor bronze brush to the cleaning rod and with short, sharp backward-and-forward movements work the brush all the way along the inside of the barrels to remove all traces of lead residue.

The barrels, when held up to a light and looked through, should be bright with no tell-tale streaks visible. To complete this stage of the cleaning, put a thin smear of oil along the inside of the barrels using the lambswool mop or a spray. Remember that the oil must be removed before the gun is used again.

Raise the extractors and with a pipe-cleaner, or a piece of cloth over a small stick, clean out any remaining powder residues.

Below are some general points that you should also be aware of:

Do not 'over-oil' a shotgun, as this can result in a 'gumming-up' of the moving parts. The parts which require the merest drop of oil from time to time are those which receive the greatest friction. On a sidelock-action it is a straightforward process to remove the locks to enable drying and cleaning of the action. With a boxlock it involves the removal of the bottom plate (positioned just forward of the trigger guard).

Whenever attempting to remove any screw, it is essential that the screwdriver is of an accurate fit to avoid damaging the screw.

If your gun has received an extensive soaking, place it in a warm, dry area with the barrels in such a position as to allow any water which has remained in the gutters alongside the rib to run off. Do not place the stock too near a direct source of heat or in too warm a place, as the wood may warp or split. Re-examine the gun the following day to make doubly sure that no rust has begun to accumulate.

When cleaning your gun, examine it for faults and/or damage.

If you are not using your gun for some time, then examine it frequently to ensure that no rust is building up while it is in storage.

When putting your gun into its case, or slip, hold the barrels with a cloth to avoid leaving sweat marks which could form the basis for rust.

Shotguns should be sent to a competent gunsmith for a clean and overhaul every year. Do this well before the season opens in order to avoid a last minute panic.

**Store your shotgun and cartridges
safely and securely**

Always check that a shotgun is unloaded immediately you handle it.

Always pass a shotgun to someone stock first with the breech open and empty.

Always treat any gun as loaded and therefore potentially dangerous.

Always ensure that the barrels are not pointed at anything which you do not intend to shoot.

Always carry a shotgun open and empty when in company.

It is not sufficient simply to believe that a shotgun is unloaded when you first handle it; it must be an automatic reaction to check that it is unloaded by opening it, if it is of the drop-down variety, or by examining the breech and chamber, if it is a pump or self-loading action gun.

Accidents have occurred when a gun was believed to be empty.

You must check.

checking that a shotgun is unloaded (*left*)

passing a shotgun stock first with the breach open and empty (*below*)

Even when you have emptied the gun or checked that it is unloaded, do not assume that safety precautions can be disregarded.

Always take special care with pump-action and self-loading guns.

In close company carry such guns with the slide or action open.

With pump-action or self-loading shotguns always take special care to ensure that there is no obstruction in the barrel.

Always ensure that any shotgun you intend to use is in a safe and sound condition.

Make certain that the internal mechanism is in a proper state of adjustment.

You must be able to recognise the following potential problems which can occur with shotguns:

Denting and/or bulging of the barrel

A dent causes a restriction in the barrel which will result in excessive pressure in the barrel. A bulge is a weakening of the structure of the barrel.

Pitting of the barrels

Pitting can occur both inside and outside barrel bores and will result in a weakening of the barrel strength. It is caused by poor care and maintenance.

Raised ribs

Raised ribs will involve a weakening of the barrel wall (if caused by rusting) and almost certainly a weakening of the barrel structure.

Damaged or cracked stocks

A cracked stock may break as a result of recoil and is a potential hazard to the shooter and anyone nearby.

A loose action

The action should be correctly aligned to the barrels to ensure that pressure is not allowed to escape when the gun is fired.

Always have your gun regularly overhauled by a competent gunsmith.

Have faults rectified immediately. A gun should be annually inspected by a gunsmith.

Always ensure that you understand the proof markings on any shotgun you use.

The law relating to the proofing of guns is to be found in the Gun Barrel Proof Acts 1868, 1950 and 1978 and in various Rules of Proof. Whilst the Acts and Rules are complex, the reason for the need to understand the proof markings on any gun you use is straightforward.

The proof marks will show whether or not a gun has been tested for particular loads and powders.

Cartridges with a heavier load than that

indicated by the proof mark should not be used.

The proof marks and explanatory notes appear in Appendix 3.

Always ensure that any gun you intend to use is safe and in proof for the cartridge you intend to use.

If any doubt exists, the gun should be examined by a gunsmith because:

1. **An unproofed gun will be in a dangerous condition and should not be used. It is a hazard not only to the user but to any other person nearby.**

2. **It is illegal to sell or offer for sale an unproofed gun. The maximum penalty is £1,000 for each offence.**

Always remember that a shotgun may be out of proof.

Always remember that there are particular problems relating to hammer guns.

Always carry hammer guns in the uncocked position, with the hammers down.

Upon the immediate expectation of a shot, cock the hammers whilst ensuring that the barrels are pointing straight upwards, placing the fingers around the outside of the trigger guard and the thumb in the crutch of the hammer.

Always open the gun before uncocking the hammers.

If you cock the hammers in the expectation of a shot but do not fire them, do not uncock the hammers onto loaded chambers.

If the right hammer in the cocked position obstructs the top lever, consult a gunsmith.

Always leave a shotgun in such a way that it cannot be knocked over or fall.

The barrels of a shotgun are made of steel, but they can easily be damaged by a knock or fall. If you must put an unloaded shotgun down, pay particular attention to where it is placed, avoiding all hazards.

Never put a loaded shotgun down.

Never mix cartridges for shotguns of different bores.

If, for example, a 20-bore cartridge is placed into the chamber of a 12-bore, it will enter the barrel far enough to allow a 12-bore cartridge to be placed above it and the gun to be closed and fired. The result will almost certainly be a burst and may be fatal.

Never allow unsupervised children to handle guns or cartridges.

Children are by nature inquisitive and want to find out about things, guns and cartridges being no exception, so lock guns and cartridges away out of reach.

Introduce youngsters to supervised correct gun-handling at an appropriate age.

SHOTGUN SAFETY IN THE HOME

Never load a shotgun indoors.

This rule is absolute. There is no reason whatsoever for loading a shotgun indoors.

Always store your shotgun and cartridges securely.

Always keep your shotguns and cartridges in separate, safe places, preferably locked away, out of sight.

A proper security cabinet is the ideal method of storing shotguns. Although it is not a legal requirement to keep shotguns under lock and key, every shotgun holder has a responsibility to himself, the police, the public and the sport to ensure adequate security precautions.

Always keep a record of shotgun serial numbers or, if there is no number, of any other distinguishing marks.

In the event of loss or theft of your shotgun this will enable you to give a full and accurate description to the police; a photograph is ideal.

SHOTGUN SAFETY WHILST TRAVELLING

Never travel with a loaded shotgun.

Before entering a vehicle check that your shotgun is unloaded. When anyone enters a vehicle with a shotgun which is not in a case or cover or you cannot see that it is empty, satisfy yourself that the gun is unloaded.

Always when travelling carry your shotgun in a case or a protective cover.

This will serve to protect the gun against any possible damage.

Always when travelling to or from a shoot ensure that your shotgun and cartridges are stored out of sight in the vehicle.

This helps to safeguard your property.

Always lock unattended vehicles.

Whenever leaving a vehicle which contains guns or cartridges, even if only for a very brief period, make certain that the vehicle is securely locked.

Always carry a shotgun so that it cannot point at anyone.

how to carry a gun over the crook of the elbow

how to carry a gun over the shoulder

NB When using the shoulder carry (*above right*), do not allow the barrels to drop towards the horizontal position. Keep the trigger guard uppermost.

Always unload your shotgun before crossing an obstacle, or negotiating difficult terrain. In company, you must:

1. Open your shotguns. **2.** Remove cartridges. **3.** One shooter passes his gun, open and stock first, to his companion. **4–5.** Having crossed the obstacle, the shooter takes both guns from his companion. **6.** The second shooter crosses the obstacle. **7.** He takes back his gun.

If a shooting companion attempts to cross an obstacle without following this procedure, politely but firmly insist that he does.

how to cross an obstacle with a companion (1–7)

Procedure when alone

Do not attempt to negotiate an obstacle without removing the cartridges from the shotgun chamber.

If possible lay the gun down, cross the obstacle and pick the gun up.

These procedures apply to fences, gates, hedges, ditches, steep banks, fallen trees, etc.

Always look through your barrels to check whenever an obstruction could have entered.

Always be certain that the gun is proofed for the cartridges you intend to use.

Always be aware of the possibility, and the consequences, of a misfire.

If there is an uncharacteristic noise or recoil from a particular shot, make certain that you look down the barrel to determine that there is no obstruction.

Always load a shotgun by placing the cartridge in the chamber and raising the stock to the barrel.

Always make sure the barrels are pointing in a safe direction when reloading.

Always keep your fingers well clear of the triggers except when taking a shot.

Always be certain of your 'Safe Arc of Fire'.

See p. 27 for an explanation of maximum effective range.

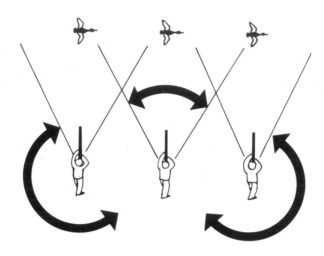

safe arc of fire

Always be aware of what is beyond your target.

Do not fire if you cannot see where the shot will go: i.e. at bushes or at a hedge. Do not fire where ricochets could occur: i.e. at rocks or water.

Details of safety procedures to be adopted whilst engaging in various aspects of the sport are discussed further in Chapter 7 (pp. 104–5) and Chapter 8 (pp. 110–111).

Always be sure of what you are shooting.

Positively identify your target before raising your shotgun to the shooting position.

SAFETY CATCHES

Always have the safety catch on 'safe' until the moment before you wish to fire.

The safety catch should not be released until the gun is mounted to the shoulder.

Always put the safety catch back on between shots. Take special care with guns without automatic safety catches.

Do not unnecessarily push the safety catch on and off whilst awaiting a shot.

The term safety catch is misleading as it does not mean that a gun cannot be fired. A mechanical device can be defective. Use the safety catch as recommended, but never handle a shotgun believing that the safety catch will stop it discharging.

how to close a shotgun

Never load a shotgun until you are about to start shooting.

Never attempt to shoot unless you are steady on your feet.

A shot taken whilst unsteady could result in the shooter losing balance at the moment of firing.

Never attach a dog's lead to yourself, whilst shooting.

If the dog is unsteady enough to require to be tied up, it may decide to move as you are about to fire, thus causing you to over-balance.

Never shoot without Third Party Liability Insurance.

Membership of the B.A.S.C. provides Third Party Liability Insurance with indemnity for up to £500,000.

Safety is a level of consciousness – not a fortunate series of events.

Safety is the responsibility of everyone – including you.

SHOTGUN CERTIFICATES IN ENGLAND, WALES AND SCOTLAND

THE SHOTGUN
CERTIFICATE
If you wish to purchase or own a shotgun, as defined in Chapter 2, you must possess a valid shotgun certificate.

Under the Firearms Act 1968 Section 2(1), if you wish to have in your possession, purchase or acquire a shotgun you must obtain a shotgun certificate from the Chief Officer of Police of the area in which you reside.

It is an offence not to do so unless you are in one of the categories listed on page 42.

shotgun certificate

Buying and selling shotguns

It is illegal (subject to limited exceptions) to buy or sell a shotgun unless both the vendor and the purchaser hold valid shotgun certificates.

HOW TO OBTAIN A
SHOTGUN CERTIFICATE

Obtain an application form from the police. Complete it and have it countersigned as described on the form.

Unless the police tell you otherwise, you should then take or send it with the appropriate fee to your local police station.

FEES FOR SHOTGUN
CERTIFICATES

The fees charged are:
On first issue   £12.00
On renewal   £ 8.00
These fees are correct at the time of going to press (December 1982), but are subject to variation by the Secretary of State.

The police will issue a receipt for your fee.

Shotgun certificates are valid for three years from the date of issue.

Certain constabularies may issue reminders to shotgun certificate holders shortly before the expiry date of the certificate. In any event, it is the shotgun certificate holder's own responsibility to renew his certificate.

CRIMINAL JUSTICE ACT 1967   Firearms Form 14

Application for the Grant of a Shot Gun Certificate

Please read the notes overleaf before completing this form.
Please write in BLOCK CAPITALS except when signing.

For Official Use

2 | Dvn | Force | Certificate Number | Date of expiry (Day | Month | Year) | Nat. Code |

1 Name of applicant ....

(Mr, Mrs, Miss or title)   Initials   Surname

2 Full postal address ....

3 Date of birth: Day | Month | Year

4 Nationality ....   5 Place of birth ....

6 Height ....   7 If married woman, surname before marriage ....

8 If the address at 2 is not your permanent one, please give permanent address below:

9 If you have lived at other addresses during the last 3 years, give them below:

10 Business address ....

11 Do you suffer from any form of mental disorder or defect?   YES / NO   *If YES, give details overleaf.*

12 Have you been convicted of ANY offence other than minor traffic offences?   YES / NO   *If YES, give details overleaf.*

13 I hereby apply to the chief officer of police for a shot gun certificate and I declare that the statements made on this form are true.

Date ....   Usual signature of applicant ....

If the applicant is under 17 years of age, signature of parent or guardian ....

14 COUNTERSIGNATURE (see note 7)

I certify that the applicant .... has been known personally to me for .... years and that, to the best of my knowledge and belief, the answers given to questions 1 to 10 above are correct. I am a British subject.

Profession or occupation ....   Signed ....

Address ....

application form

CONDITIONS OF ISSUE

A shotgun certificate is issued subject to the following conditions:
1. The holder must, on receipt of the certificate, sign it in ink with his usual signature.
2. The holder of a shotgun certificate must immediately inform the Chief Officer of the police force by whom it was granted of the theft or loss in Great Britain of any shotgun in his possession.

THEFT OR LOSS OF A SHOTGUN CERTIFICATE

Since it is illegal to possess a shotgun unless you hold a certificate, you must immediately inform the Chief Officer of the police force by whom it was granted if you lose your shotgun certificate or have it stolen. If you do not do so you may be guilty of an offence.

The fee for a replacement certificate is £8 (as at December 1982).

Although it is not a condition of issue, it is stated on the shotgun certificate that you should notify the Chief Officer of the police force which issued the certificate of any change of address, and send your certificate for replacement.

Failure to do so may lead to delay in renewal.

As stated above, certain categories of persons do not require a shotgun certificate. These are:

1. A person carrying a firearm (including shotgun) or ammunition belonging to another person holding a certificate under the Firearms Act 1968 may, without himself holding such a certificate, have in his possession that firearm or ammunition under instructions from that other person and for the use of that other person for sporting purposes only.

This may be interpreted to include for example a loader.

2. A person may, without holding a shotgun certificate, borrow a shotgun from the occupier of private premises (including private land) and use it on those premises in the occupier's presence.

3. A person may, without holding a shotgun certificate, use a shotgun at a time and place approved for shooting at artificial targets by the Chief Officer of the police force for the area in which that place is situated.

This may be interpreted to include a shooting school or clay-pigeon shooting ground.

4. A person who has been in Great Britain for not more than thirty days in all in the preceding twelve months may have in his possession, or purchase, or acquire a shotgun without holding a shotgun certificate.

5. A person does not commit an offence if he has in his possession, purchases, or acquires a shotgun if he holds a firearms certificate issued in Northern Ireland authorising him to possess a shotgun (see below).

FIREARMS CERTIFICATES IN NORTHERN IRELAND

REQUIREMENT FOR A
CERTIFICATE

Under the Firearms (Northern Ireland) Order 1981, if you wish to have in your possession, purchase, or acquire a shotgun you must obtain authorisation from the Chief Constable, Royal Ulster Constabulary, Brooklyn, Knock Road, Belfast BT5 6LE.

There is no distinction between shotgun, rifle or pistol in Northern Ireland. Certification is dealt with on a single form, regulated and controlled by the R.U.C. The authorised possession of a Northern Ireland firearms certificate exempts the holder from holding a shotgun certificate in England, Scotland and Wales.

FEES FOR NORTHERN
IRELAND

The current fees are:
On the issue of a new certificate   £21.00
For renewal, variation or replacement thereafter   £13.25
N.B. These fees are correct at the time of going to press (December 1982), but may be varied by Parliament.

It is not an offence under the Order for any person to have in his possession a firearm (including a shotgun) or ammunition if he can show that by virtue of the Order he is entitled to have possession of the firearm without holding a certificate.

For example: Section 12 (1) permits a person to carry a firearm or ammunition belonging to another person holding a firearms certificate, without himself holding such a certificate, and to have in his possession that firearm or ammunition under instructions from and for the use of that other person for sporting purposes only.

Persons holding valid certificates granted in Great Britain will be exempt from acquiring the equivalent certificate in Northern Ireland. (Section 15.)

THE ACQUISITION AND POSSESSION OF SHOTGUNS BY PERSONS UNDER THE AGE OF 18

THE PURCHASE,
POSSESSION AND USE OF
SHOTGUNS BY JUNIORS IN
ENGLAND, SCOTLAND
AND WALES

There is no lower age limit for possession of a shotgun certificate, but there are limitations on the age at which juniors may possess or purchase shotguns and ammunition.

UNDER 15 YEARS OLD

It is an offence to make a gift of a shotgun or ammunition to a person under 15 years old.

A person under 15 may not have an assembled shotgun with him except:
(i) when he is under the direct supervision of someone of or over 21, in which case he may use the shotgun, providing he has a valid shotgun certificate, under that person's instructions;
(ii) when the shotgun is in a securely fastened gun cover so that it cannot be fired.

AGED 15–17

A person between 15 and 17 years old may be given or lent a shotgun and ammunition, but he may not buy them.

After reaching the age of 15, a person may use a shotgun without supervision providing he holds a valid shotgun certificate.

AGE 17

On reaching the age of 17 a person may purchase a shotgun providing he holds a valid shotgun certificate, and he may buy ammunition.

JUNIORS IN NORTHERN
IRELAND

Subject to the exceptions listed below, a person who being under the age of eighteen years, purchases, acquires or has in his possession a firearm or ammunition shall be guilty of an offence. (Firearms (N.I.) Order 1981. Section 26 (1).)

It is not an offence for any person not being under the age of 16 years old

(*a*) to have with him a firearm (including a shotgun) or ammunition for sporting purposes when he is in the company, and under the supervision of another person not under the age of 18 who holds a firearms certificate in respect of that firearm or ammunition;

(*b*) to purchase, acquire or have in his possession a shotgun, or any other firearm of a calibre not exceeding .22in, and ammunition therefore for the purpose of destroying or controlling animals and birds:

(*i*) on agricultural lands occupied by him;

(*ii*) on agricultural lands on which he works and on which he also resides.

POLICE POWERS

When out shooting, carry your shotgun certificate with you. A constable may demand from any person whom he believes to be in possession of a shotgun, the production of his shotgun certificate.

If a person upon whom a demand is made fails to produce the certificate or to permit the constable to read it, or to show that he is entitled by virtue of the Act to have the shotgun in his possession without holding a certificate, the constable may seize and detain the shotgun and may require the person to declare to him immediately his name and address.

If under this section of the Firearms Act a person is required to give his name and address to a constable, it is an offence for him to refuse to declare it or to fail to give his true name and address.

APPEALS AGAINST POLICE DECISION TO REFUSE TO ISSUE OR RENEW A SHOTGUN CERTIFICATE

ENGLAND AND WALES

If the police refuse to grant, vary or renew your shotgun certificate, you may appeal to the Crown Court on giving notice within twenty-one days of the refusal to the clerk of the court and the Chief Officer of the police force for the area.

SCOTLAND

In Scotland you may appeal to the Sheriff.

NORTHERN IRELAND

In Northern Ireland you may appeal to the Secretary of State.

SHOTGUNS IN PUBLIC PLACES

A person commits an offence if, without lawful authority or reasonable excuse (the proof whereof lies on him), he has with him in a public place a loaded shotgun.

Public place includes any highway or any other premises or place to which the public has access at the time in question and includes land covered by water.

TRESPASS

A person commits an offence if while he has a firearm (this includes a shotgun) with him, he enters or is on any land as a trespasser and without reasonable excuse (the proof whereof lies on him).

A person commits an offence if, while he has a firearm (this includes a shotgun) with him, he enters or is in any building or part of a building as a trespasser and without reasonable excuse (the proof whereof lies on him).

SHOOTING ON OR NEAR A HIGHWAY

It is an offence without lawful authority or reasonable excuse to shoot within fifty feet of the centre of a highway if in consequence someone on the highway is injured, interfered with or endangered.

FOOTPATHS AND BRIDLEWAYS

A person having the right to shoot on land over which a right of way (footpath or bridleway) passes has lawful authority and reasonable excuse to have a loaded shotgun on or near the footpath or bridleway.

THE USE OF SHOTGUNS IN RELATION TO THE WILDLIFE AND COUNTRYSIDE ACT 1981

THE PROTECTION OF WILD BIRDS

The Wildlife and Countryside Act 1981 protects all wild birds (except those covered by the Game Acts), their nests and eggs, subject to clearly defined exceptions.

These exceptions provide for open seasons during which certain species may be shot, and they lift restrictions on shooting certain 'pest' species throughout the year.

Remember that all species are protected: some receive special protection all year or during the close season.

Penalties for killing or harming otherwise protected species are severe.

THE QUARRY SPECIES

The species which may be shot during the open season (see below for details of the seasons) are listed in Schedule 2 Part I in Appendix 4.

The species which are commonly regarded as 'pest species' and which may be shot by 'authorised persons' (see below) throughout the year are listed in Schedule 2 Part II in Appendix 4.

AUTHORISED PERSONS

Under the Wildlife and Countryside Act, 'authorised persons' means:
(a) the owner or occupier, or any person authorised by the owner or occupier, of the land on which the action authorised is taken;

45

(b) any person authorised in writing by the local authority for the area within which the action authorised is taken;

(c) any person authorised in writing by the Nature Conservancy Council, a water authority, or a local fisheries committee constituted under the Sea Fisheries Regulations Act 1966;

but with the proviso that the authorisation of any person for the purposes of this definition shall not confer any right of entry upon any land.

RACING PIGEONS

Racing pigeons are not listed in the Schedules, but may not be shot or taken at any time.

THE OPEN SEASONS

The seasons during which certain birds may be killed or taken are as follows:

Capercaillie and (except in Scotland)
  Woodcock: 1 October–31 January (inclusive)
Woodcock in Scotland: 1 September–31 January (inc)
Snipe, Common: 12 August–31 January (inc)
Wild Duck and Geese inland: 1 September–31 January (inc)
  on the foreshore: 1 September–20 February (inc)
Other species in Schedule 2 Part I
  (Coot, Moorhen):   1 September–31 January (inc)

It is illegal to shoot Schedule 2 birds on Christmas Day in England, Scotland and Wales, and on Sundays in Scotland and certain counties in England and Wales. (These are listed on p. 116.)

The seasons for game birds appear on pages 49–50.

PERIODS OF SPECIAL
PROTECTION

Under exceptional circumstances, for example prolonged severe weather or serious pollution, the Secretary of State may protect by order any species of wild bird included in Schedule 1 Part II or Schedule 2 Part I for periods of not more than fourteen days. He will act in accordance with criteria and procedures previously agreed by Government, sporting and conservation organisations. Before making such an order, the Secretary of State shall consult a person appearing to him to be a representative of persons interested in the shooting of birds of the kind proposed to be protected by the order.

PROHIBITED METHODS
OF TAKING/KILLING
WILD BIRDS, INCLUDING
GAME

The following methods (relating to the use of shotguns) of killing or taking wild birds, are prohibited:

1. By using any automatic or semi-automatic weapon.

'Automatic weapon' and 'semi-automatic weapon' do not include any weapon the magazine of which is incapable of holding more than two rounds.

2. Any shotgun of which the barrel has an internal diameter at the muzzle of more than one and three-quarter inches.

3. The use of any device for illuminating a target.

4. The use of any form of artificial lighting or any mirror or other dazzling device.

5. The use as a decoy of any sound recording, or any live bird, or animal which is tethered, or which is secured by means of braces or other similar appliances, or which is blind, maimed or injured.

6. **The use of any mechanically propelled vehicle in immediate pursuit of a wild bird for the purpose of killing or taking that bird.**

KILLING CERTAIN
SPECIES CAUSING
DAMAGE

The Act makes provision for an authorised person to shoot any wild bird (other than the species in Schedule 1 – see Appendix 4) if he can show that his action was necessary for preventing serious damage to crops, livestock or fisheries.

Otherwise, the shooting of certain other species which may cause damage is controlled under licence.

The B.A.S.C. will provide information on licence arrangements on request.

THE SALE OF DEAD WILD
BIRDS

Generally the sale of dead wild birds is prohibited, but the sale of the following species (Schedule 3 Part II) is allowed at all times:
Pigeon, Feral
Woodpigeon

The sale of the following dead wild birds (Schedule 3 Part III) is allowed during the period 1 September–28 February only:

Capercaillie	Pochard
Coot	Shoveler
Duck, Tufted	Snipe, Common
Mallard	Teal
Pintail	Wigeon
Plover, Golden	Woodcock

THE PROTECTION OF WILD ANIMALS

The Wildlife and Countryside Act 1981 provides protection to wild animals and lists in Schedule 5 (see Appendix 4) those species which are specifically protected. These species are unlikely to be encountered whilst shooting, except for the Red Squirrel, bats and the Otter.

Excluded methods for killing or taking any wild animal

It is illegal, however, to use certain methods for killing or taking any wild animals. The sporting shotgun shooter should be aware that he is guilty of an offence if he:

(*i*) uses for the purpose of killing or taking any wild animal any self-locking snare, any bow or crossbow or any explosive other than ammunition for a firearm (including shotgun);

(*ii*) uses as a decoy, for the purpose of killing or taking any wild animal, any live mammal or bird.

Excluded methods for
killing or taking Schedule 6
animals

Additionally, animals which appear in Schedule 6 may not be killed or taken by the following methods:

1. **Any automatic or semi-automatic weapon.**
2. **Any device for illuminating a target or sighting device for nightshooting.**
3. **Any form of artificial light or any mirror or other dazzling device.**
4. **Use as a decoy, for the purpose of killing or taking any such wild animal, any sound recording.**
5. **Using any mechanically propelled vehicle in immediate pursuit of any such wild animal for the purpose of driving, killing or taking that animal.**

The above methods 1–5 are by implication permitted for the purpose of taking or killing those animals which do not appear in Schedules 5 or 6.

SCHEDULE 6

Animals in Schedule 6 which are likely to be encountered whilst shooting:

Badger	Marten, Pine
Bats (all species)	Otter, Common
Cat, Wild	Polecat
Hedgehog	Squirrel, Red

NORTHERN IRELAND

THE SEASONS AND THE SCHEDULES

All birds, their eggs and nests are protected at all times by the Protection of Birds Act 1954.

NOTE: This will be superseded by the Wildlife and Countryside Act when a Northern Ireland Order is prepared and passed.

The Act, however, makes provision for certain species to be killed or taken at certain times by authorised persons.

Category I Birds

Birds in Category I may be killed or taken at any time by authorised persons. These are:

Shag	Crow, Carrion
Cormorant	Rook
Swan, Mute	Jackdaw
Gull, Great Black-backed	Magpie
Gull, Lesser Black-backed	Jay
Gull, Herring	Starling
Gull, Black-headed	Bullfinch
Woodpigeon	Sparrow, House
Crow, Hooded	

Category II Birds

Birds in Category II are specially protected at all times subject to the following limited exceptions:

Pigeon, Feral	Chaffinch
Blackbird	Greenfinch

The above birds may be taken when it is necessary for the

owner or occupier of any land, or a person or persons authorised in writing signed by him to act on his behalf, to kill or take these birds on the land of the owner or occupier in order to protect the crops or property.

The eggs and nests of these birds shall be specially protected at all times.

Category III Birds

Birds in Category III are specially protected during the close season but may be taken or killed by authorised persons during the open season (1 September–31 January).

Their eggs and nest are protected at all times.

The birds in Category III are:

Geese (all species)	Dove, Stock
Ducks (all species)	Redshank
Plover, Golden	Curlew

The Mute Swan, Whimbrel and Rock Dove are presently (1982) included in this category, but will be subject to change by the Wildlife and Countryside Act 1981 when a Northern Ireland Order is prepared and passed.

Barnacle, Brent and Canada Geese

Barnacle, Brent and Canada Geese, and their eggs and nests are specially protected at all times subject to review, 1972 S.R. & O. (N.I.) 1969 No. 216.

THE SHOOTING SEASONS IN NORTHERN IRELAND

THE OPEN AND CLOSE SEASONS FOR GAME AND WILDFOWL

Grouse,	12 August–30 November inclusive.
Pheasant*,	1 October–31 January inclusive.
Wild ducks and Wild geese†,	1 September–31 January inclusive.

Woodcock, Snipe Common, Redshank, Curlew Common,

Golden Plover,	1 September–31 January inclusive.
Hares,	12 August–31 January inclusive.

Partridge – Fully protected at all times.
*Hen pheasant protected.
†Barnacle, Brent and Canada geese are protected.

THE GAME ACTS

ENGLAND, SCOTLAND AND WALES

'Game' includes hares, pheasants, partridges, grouse, heath or moor game and black game.

THE GAME SEASONS

Pheasant	1 October – 1 February inclusive
Partridge	1 September – 1 February inclusive
Grouse/Ptarmigan	12 August – 10 December inclusive
Blackgame	20 August – 10 December inclusive
Hare	No season but may not be offered for sale from 1 March – 31 July inclusive

It is illegal to shoot any species out of season.

It is illegal to shoot game on Sundays, Christmas Day or at night.

Game Licences

It is illegal to shoot all game species, Common Snipe and Woodcock without a Game Licence (but certain exceptions apply in the case of Hares – see below).

Cost of Game Licences

£6.00 for annual licence expiry 31 July.
£4.00 for the period 1 August – 31 October.
£4.00 for the period 1 November – 31 July.
£2.00 for a period of 14 days.
Game licences are available at any Crown Post Office.

Gamekeeper's Licence

A Gamekeeper's Licence to authorise a gamekeeper to kill game costs £4.00.

Game Dealer's Licence

A Game Dealer's Licence costs £4.00.

It is an offence to sell game without a licence.

Only a licensed dealer or a person having a licence to kill game may sell game; the latter only to a licensed game dealer. A gamekeeper with a Gamekeeper's Licence and his employer's written permission may sell game on behalf of his employer to a licensed game dealer.

There is a penalty not exceeding £5 when persons not licensed to deal buy from other than a licensed dealer; for example, guns buying an extra brace from the shoot owner who is not a licensed dealer.

An occupier of land may, under the provision of the Ground Game Act, sell hares killed on his land without either having a licence to kill or a licence to deal in, but only to a licensed dealer.

A Dealer's Licence is obtainable from the local Council; when this has been issued a further licence (cost £4.00) must be obtained from a Money Order Post Office. Two licences are needed, one under the Game Act 1831 and the other an Excise Licence under the Game Licence Act 1860.

Hares

You do not require a Game Licence to shoot hares, provided that you are shooting on land where you are the owner (having the right to kill game), occupier or a person duly authorised in writing under the provisions of either the Hares Act 1848 or the Ground Game Acts.

Only one person can be so authorised and must be either:

1. A member of the occupier's household resident on the land;
2. A person in the occupier's ordinary service on the land;
3. A person genuinely employed for reward to kill and take hares and rabbits on the land.

NIGHT SHOOTING

Night is taken to mean the period from one hour after sunset to one hour before sunrise.

England and Wales

Rabbits may be shot at night by the landowner or by persons authorised by him.
    Hares may be shot at night by authorised persons.
    Game may not be shot at night.

Scotland

Rabbits and Hares may be shot at night by authorised persons.
    Game may not be shot at night.

Northern Ireland

It is illegal to shoot at night.

THE LAW RELATING TO LAND OWNERSHIP

Free Shooting

There is very little free shooting in this country, shooting rights will almost always be held by the landowner or shooting tenant and under a measure of control.

If you shoot anywhere without permission, you lay yourself open to prosecution for armed trespass or trespass in pursuit of game (poaching).

According to the circumstances, you can be charged with one or both of these offences.

Always ensure that you are authorised to shoot where you intend to go.

Wildfowling on the foreshore is often thought to be free shooting. It is not. The law, and the exceptions, are explained in detail in Chapter 9.

Whether peer or postman, tipster or tycoon,
Heed these words of warning otherwise you'll soon
Realise what happens in most every court –
'Ignorance of Law' can mean 'Farewell to your Sport'.

ANON

5 Behaviour in the Field

The following is a code of conduct regarding behaviour when in the field. More specific references to conduct when engaged in game shooting, wildfowling, and roughshooting occur in the respective sections.

Always remember that others will judge the sport by your behaviour and that of your companions.

If you observe others behaving in a manner likely to bring the sport into disrepute, politely but firmly bring their responsibility to the sport as a whole to their attention.

Always remember your responsibility to safeguard your quarry and its habitat for future generations.

Know the quarry species and their respective seasons.

Always ensure that you are authorised to shoot where you intend to go.

You must know precisely where the shoot boundaries are located.

Know the location of any public rights of way in the area.

Always advise the owner and/or the tenant in good time if you want to go shooting.

Check that it is convenient for you to go shooting at the time you intend to go. Check for restrictions which might affect your sport.

Always avoid causing unnecessary disturbance.

Avoid shooting at night where noise may be a nuisance.

Always respect the owner's property.

Respect crops, livestock, property and fences; damage to property may result in a loss of shooting rights.

Always open gates rather than climb them. Close gates after you, if they were closed initially. You may cut stock off from water by closing a gate intentionally left open. Climb a secured gate at the hinged end.

Do not break fences, rails or hedges.

Do not walk in standing corn; seek the farmer's guidance in respect of other growing crops.

Avoid disturbance to livestock.

Always keep your dog under control.

Do not let your dog disturb livestock. Sheep in lamb can be harmed if made to run; a dog need not chase sheep to cause them to panic. Schedule 7 of the Wildlife and Countryside Act 1981 and the Dogs (Protection of Livestock) Act 1953 make provision for the incurring of a penalty in law if a dog is allowed to worry livestock on agricultural ground or is at large (that is, not on a lead or otherwise under close control) in a field or enclosure in which there are sheep.

If quarry is shot and falls or runs over the boundary, it is proper to seek permission to retrieve it.

Always observe the B.A.S.C. Shotgun Safety Code.

This is outlined in detail in Chapter 3. You should be thoroughly conversant with this.

Always remember that it is the sportsman's responsibility to understand the laws relating to his sport.

You must be aware of the laws relating to the sport, particularly to shotguns and to your quarry (see Chapter 4).

Always seek to present your quarry as a sporting shot.

Allow flushed quarry to gain reasonable distance (14m/approximately 15yd).
   Remember that it is equally unsporting to shoot at quarry which is out of range. Vermin shooting may be excepted in the case of close shots, **but out-of-range shooting at vermin is also inexcusable.**

Always ensure that your shooting is as good as possible.

You will improve your shooting by practice on clay pigeons. One recommended method of shooting a moving target is given in Appendix 5.

Always 'mark' by carefully watching wounded game and ensure that it is picked up without delay.

A trained gundog is recommended whenever you shoot.
   Every conceivable effort should be made to locate, pick up and humanely despatch wounded quarry.

Always despatch wounded quarry as humanely and as quickly as possible.

A sharp knock on the head with a suitably heavy stick or 'priest' is most effective for birds.
   Hares and rabbits can be killed by holding them by the head between the first and second fingers, with the first finger extended under the creature's chin, and quickly jerking the animal downwards, effecting a dislocation of the neck by the weight of the body.

Always observe the Code of Practice for safe gun-handling when despatching wounded quarry.

Always wear suitable and sensible clothing and footwear to suit your surroundings.

Make contingency plans for wet and cold weather and carry appropriate clothing.

Always ensure that your shotgun certificate is signed and valid.

Always ensure that you have a valid game licence if shooting at game.

Carry it and your shotgun certificate whenever you go out shooting.

Always take your quarry from the game bag as soon as possible.

Store it in a cool, fly-proof place. Do not waste it.

Always remember that the enjoyment of sport is not reflected by the size of the bag.

Do not over shoot. A viable breeding stock must be left on the ground at the end of the season. (Crop protection may be an exception.)

Never shoot a bird just because it is within range of your gun.

Although it may be in range of your gun, it may provide a more sporting shot for another gun.

Never leave litter.

Take all your litter home with you. This includes empty cartridge cases.

Whenever possible pick up litter left by someone else. Litter can be a hazard to livestock.

Never let excitement cloud your judgement.

Concentration and attention to safety are vital at all times.

The sportsman's responsibility is to ensure that he positively identifies his target before taking a shot.

It is essential that the sportsman should be able to distinguish rapidly between quarry and non-quarry species in the field. The primary aim of this guide is to help sportsmen to learn the techniques of species identification, with particular reference to the main quarry species. But the principles established apply equally to non-quarry species. Through practising field identification at every opportunity the sportsman will not only become competent at recognising his target species, he will also benefit from his ability to identify non-quarry animals.

Species identification is a craft, the skills for which are acquired through field experience.

It is important for the sportsman to have access to guides and texts to help him learn the characteristic field marks of both quarry and non-quarry species. It is equally important for him to appreciate that no amount of 'armchair identification' can substitute for field experience. This section is no more than an introductory guide. It is necessarily limited in scope, and covers only the most popular sporting quarry species. It should be supplemented by extensive practice of quarry identification under a wide range of field conditions, and used in conjunction with a more comprehensive field guide (a selection of the more popular field guides are listed on page 56). These field guides will help the sportsman to become more aware of non-quarry species—including those which occur in Britain only occasionally or in very small numbers. The experience gained through attempting to identify all species encountered, regardless of their quarry status and throughout the year, will enhance the sportsman's enjoyment of the countryside and eliminate the risks of shooting at non-quarry species.

HOW TO IDENTIFY QUARRY SPECIES

The aim of this guide is to establish the basic principles which enable the sportsman to recognise quarry species.

Quarry species comprise two groups of animals—birds and mammals. The features used to recognise the differences between these two groups of animals can be used to illustrate the basic principles of species identification. Birds are immediately recognisable by their feathers and wings, and mammals by their fur and four limbs. Species identification is simply an extension of the ability to recognise features which tell apart different species. Most people will almost instinctively be able to 'identify' an animal as being a bird or mammal—and many will be able to go one step further and define the type of, say, bird as a 'duck' or a 'pigeon'. Species identification is achieved through learning the key field-marks and behaviour which characterise particular groups and species from one another, and enable the animal under observation to be positively identified.

The features which provide the most useful clues to quarry identification are the animal's size, shape, markings, colour, general behaviour and distribution in both space and time.

Positive species identification usually results from a combination of the various diagnostic features.

The features which provide the most useful clues to quarry recognition are:

1. Size and shape
It is particularly important to use a familiar species as a guide for comparison with other species in the same group; and also to note any distinctive features of the animal's shape which permit identification in silhouette, including, in the case of birds, those features which are readily seen in flight.

2. Colour and pattern
Note any unique colouring, or patterns of colour, paying particular attention to markings which can be detected at long range.

3. Behaviour
Visual clues, such as the way an animal moves on the ground, a bird's flight or perching behaviour, and audible signals such as call-notes or the sounds created by wing-beats are all important in species recognition.

4. Habitat and seasonal pattern
As all species show some kind of preference where they feed or seek shelter, the kind of habitat gives some indication of the species which might be found in a particular area.

Knowledge of species' habitat preferences taken together with any seasonal migration movements enables the sportsman to anticipate, within broad limits, which species he is likely to encounter at a particular locality. But general distribution limits—such as 'normal' habitat and 'usual' range for example—cannot be used alone as diagnostic features.

Further reading

The list below contains a small selection from the wide range of field guides and other texts which will give the sportsman more information and guidance on the identification of British birds and mammals, and on the natural history of the main quarry species. Most of these books are inexpensive and widely available from bookshops.

FIELD IDENTIFICATION GUIDES

Birds

Hermann Heinzel, Richard Fitter and John Parslow: *The Birds of Britain and Europe*, Collins, London.
P.A.D. Hollom: *The Popular Handbook of British Birds*, Witherby, London.
Roger Peterson, Guy Mountfort and P. A. D. Hollom: *A Field Guide to the Birds of Britain and Europe*, Collins, London.

Mammals

G. B. Corbet and H. N. Southern: *The Handbook of British Mammals*, Blackwell, Oxford.

M. J. Lawrence and R. W. Brown: *Mammals of Britain: Their Tracks, Trails and Signs*, Blandford, Poole.

Specialised texts

Franklin Coombs: *The Crows*, Batsford, London.
M. A. Ogilvie: *Ducks of Britain and Europe*, Poyser, Berkhamsted.
Myrfyn Owen: *Wild Geese of the World*, Batsford, London.
A. J. Prater: *Estuary Birds of Britain and Ireland*, Poyser, Calton.

THE QUARRY SPECIES

The 35 most popular quarry animals which may, under current legislation, be pursued for sport by authorised persons are described in detail in this section.

Current legislation provides for open shooting seasons or shooting by authorised persons of 80 species of wild birds and terrestrial mammals in Britain. This includes both traditional sporting quarry species (wildfowl, gamebirds, hares, etc) and animals shot for pest control purposes (some gulls, rats and mustelids—stoats, weasels, etc), together with some species which fall into a grey area between the two categories (including crows, Woodpigeon and Rabbit).

Those animals regarded primarily as pest species are outside the scope of this volume, which is concerned only with the sporting quarry which may be taken with a shotgun. Thus, of the 38 birds which may be shot, the Great and Lesser Black-backed and Herring Gulls, Collared Dove, Feral Pigeon, Starling and House Sparrow are excluded. Of the mammals, only four species are considered to be targets for sporting shotgun shooting. Full details of the legal framework for shotgun shooting are given in Chapter 4 (The Law) and Appendix 4 to which the reader is referred for further information.

Quarry animals fall into several categories of similar species.

The 35 quarry animals (31 birds and 4 mammals) are grouped into the following categories of similar or closely related species.

WILDFOWL

These comprise ducks and geese, large numbers of which are migratory, visiting the British Isles during autumn and winter, returning in spring to northern breeding grounds.

Ducks

These are the most widespread and numerous wildfowl. Sexes are normally very dissimilar—the male (drake) is usually highly coloured, except in eclipse plumage, while the female (duck) has characteristically drab plumage throughout the year. The nine quarry species of ducks can be usefully divided in two groups according to their mode of feeding.

57

1. Dabbling ducks

This group comprises Mallard, Teal, Wigeon, Pintail, Shoveler and Gadwall. As their group name suggests, dabblers obtain food mainly from shallow water, paddling to stir up mud, etc. or 'up-ending' to sieve out food material from just below the surface. They tend to be agile on land. Mallard, Teal and Gadwall regularly feed on agricultural land, especially cereal stubbles in autumn; while Wigeon chiefly graze on grassland.

Species in this group are typified by the ease with which they take to the wing—an important escape strategy as birds frequently feed in small wetlands, damp woodlands, etc. Teal will rise almost vertically from the surface. All fly easily and show considerable agility on the wing.

Most dabblers are typically night-feeders. Their normal pattern is to use a safe roost site during the day, frequently on open water such as small- to medium-sized ponds, and flight to feeding areas at dusk, returning to their roost at dawn. This generalised pattern may be complicated by local weather and feeding conditions and will vary with different species. Those feeding on the foreshore, such as Wigeon grazing saltings, are governed largely by tidal cycles. Bright moonlight (which can occur under clear skies during full moon) resembles daylight and can result in a complex pattern of movements between roost site and intertidal feeding areas. This period of bright moonlit nights is also exploited by inland ducks which similarly flight between roost and feeding areas during the night.

2. Diving ducks

This group comprises Tufted Duck, Pochard and Goldeneye.

These species typically use deeper, open waters for both feeding and roosting, and one site can fulfil both functions. They dive to moderate depths to forage on plant or animal material from the water or bottom muds. Ducks in this group are highly adapted to swimming and as a result they move with less ease on land than dabbling ducks. They are also slower in taking to the wing, and have to patter along the surface to gain lift. Often they will swim away or dive to avoid danger, only taking flight as a last resort. They do flight to and from roost sites if these differ from feeding waters; and they often show a peak of activity in evening and early morning, resting in the middle of the night.

Geese

This group includes Britain's largest quarry bird species. They are divided into two groups. The 'grey' geese (*Anser* species) are Greylag, Pink-footed and White-fronted; they are basically grey and greyish-brown with typically fairly uniform plumage tones. The 'black' or 'dark' geese (*Branta* species) tend to have a contrasting black or dark brown with white or light grey colouring; the Canada Goose is the only quarry species in this group. Sexes are generally similar, and indistinguishable in the field. The young of all grey geese look rather similar, generally lacking adult plumage characters, but as they tend to retain strong family ties during their first winter problems of identification are reduced. Geese typically feed during the day and roost at night; although, as with ducks, tidal cycles and moonlight will alter patterns of movement, especially of those species using tidal areas for feeding. Flocks (skeins) normally fly in V-formation or straggly lines. Their call notes are highly characteristic, and hence are very important in species recognition.

OTHER WATERBIRDS

Two species of the rail family—Moorhen and Coot—are found in a wide range of marsh and open water habitats. They are typified by bulky bodies and swim with a jerky action.

WADERS

Waders are a diverse group of birds. Golden Plover and Snipe occur in coastal marshes, inland wetlands and moors. The Woodcock is regarded as a 'forest wader' in view of its affinity to woodland habitats and close relationship to snipe. Sexes are generally indistinguishable in the field.

GAMEBIRDS

Gamebirds comprise two main groups, divided according to their habitat preferences. All gamebirds are characterised by their mode of flight. They are largely ground-dwelling birds, and tend to fly only when forced to do so. When flushed from cover they take off noisily. Once airborne their flight is strong, direct and often high, characterised by short bursts of whirring wing-beats alternating with gliding on down-curved wings.

Lowland gamebirds

These are Pheasant, Grey and Red-legged Partridges. Grey Partridge is native to Britain; the others are introduced species. All are closely associated with lowland agricultural and woodland habitats. Pheasant and Red-legged Partridges are intensively managed to maintain high populations for sporting shooting purposes. This involves both habitat management (e.g. provision of cover) and species management (e.g. rearing and release of young, providing supplementary food etc). Grey Partridge populations are managed largely through the provision of suitable cover and forage.

Upland gamebirds

This group comprises four indigenous grouse species—Red and Black Grouse, Ptarmigan and Capercaillie. The last species was

previously extinct but was re-established from breeding stock introduced from Sweden during the nineteenth century. All four species have quite distinct and different habitat requirements. Red Grouse are characteristic of open heather moors; Capercaillie inhabit upland woodland—mainly pine forest; Black Grouse are found typically in moorland and forest-edge habitats and Ptarmigan on higher, rocky mountain tops.

PIGEONS AND DOVES

Three species are legal quarry, but only the Woodpigeon is considered to be a popular target for sport-shooting. It is frequently regarded as a pest by farmers in view of the large numbers which may congregate to feed on ripening or recently sown crops.

CORVIDS

The quarry species comprise Crow (which occurs as two distinct sub-species—Carrion and Hooded), Rook, Jackdaw, Magpie and Jay.

The crow family includes species which have long been regarded as a menace to game-rearing operations. Most are considered also to be popular sporting quarry. They have a varied diet, and readily adapt to exploit available food resources—hence the problems resulting from their predation on eggs and young birds in game-rearing sites. Sexes are similar, and indistinguishable in the field. Most populations are resident, but in some areas they undertake short movements outside the breeding season to avoid harsh weather, or involving the dispersal of young.

HARE AND RABBIT

These closely related herbivores are characterised by their long hind-legs and long ears. They are capable of high speed and rapid changes in direction while running.

The Brown and Mountain Hares are traditionally considered as game species. The Rabbit is frequently regarded as a pest species, but is also a sporting quarry.

SQUIRRELS

The Grey Squirrel is the only quarry species in this group. It is characterised by its long tail and arboreal habits. It is considered a sporting quarry, although it is most frequently shot to prevent damage to forestry and game interests.

USING THE QUARRY IDENTIFICATION GUIDE

Each species description concentrates on the features which enable the sportsman to make a positive identification of his quarry, together with information on its normal range and habitat preferences. A glossary of technical terms is given opposite.

BIRD TOPOGRAPHY

The parts of a bird referred to in the species accounts are labelled on the fictitious bird illustrated on this page. The annotated features are defined in the list below together with some aspects of plumage or anatomy which are not depicted on the diagram.

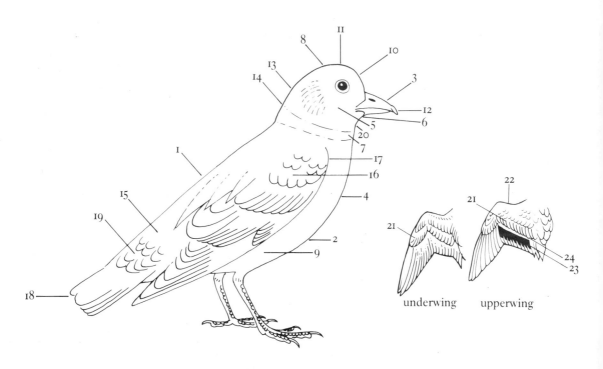

underwing   upperwing

Profile diagram

1 Back	10 Forehead	19 Tail coverts
2 Belly	11 Head	20 Throat
3 Bill	12 Nail	
4 Breast (Chest)	13 Nape	
5 Cheek	14 Neck	*Wing Detail*
6 Chin	15 Rump	21 Coverts
7 Collar	16 Scapulars	22 Forewing
8 Crown	17 Shoulder	23 Speculum
9 Flank	18 Tail	24 Wing-bar

Features not illustrated
Frontal shield: hard, bare plate extending from top of bill over forehead.
Wattle: an area of bare, usually bright coloured flesh below throat.

The more technical terms used, mainly in connection with behaviour or habitat, are defined.

Arboreal tree-dwelling species.

Brackish intermediate between fresh and salt (sea) water.

Crepuscular active during twilight hours.

Diurnal active during daylight hours.

Eclipse the dull plumage of adult male ducks in late summer, at which time they are rendered temporarily flightless as they moult their flight feathers.

Feral wild population originating from introduced stocks (released or escaped animals).

Form shallow depression or 'nest'-scrape of hares.

Gregarious found in association with others of the same species.

Herbivore species which feeds by grazing vegetation.

Lek traditional site for male courtship displays during spring.

Maritime coastal environment.

Migrant a species whose regular movement between summer (breeding) range and wintering grounds involves a substantial part of the population crossing national frontiers; 'passage migrant' describes a species which passes through a country en route between the countries in which its breeding and wintering grounds are located.

Moult loss and renewal of bird's feathers—normally occurs at least once each year. (See also *Eclipse*.)

Moult-migration movement of birds to areas where they can moult safely—applies in particular to ducks and geese with temporary flightless period.

Nocturnal active during hours of darkness.

Passage migrant (see under *Migrant*).

Predator species which kills individuals of other species for food.

Resident species remaining within the same country (but not necessarily the same locality) throughout the year.

Roding courtship behaviour of male Woodcock patrolling breeding habitat during spring and summer.

Roost main period of rest in a bird's 24-hour cycle of activity (not necessarily involving true sleep, and frequently during daylight as well as at night); also describes the place where birds settle to rest.

Saline salt water.

Sedentary species in which individuals normally remain in the same locality throughout the year.

Solitary normally found alone (or in breeding season as isolated pairs).

Terrestrial land-dwelling.

QUARRY SPECIES

In the following species descriptions, the vernacular (common) name of each species is followed by its scientific (Latin) name. Size refers to the average length of the adult animal from tip of its bill/nose to tail, with ranges given for species with marked size variation or significant differences between the sexes. Each species is shown in full colour.

To aid flight identification, monochrome figures of ducks in flight are included with each species description, and normal flock patterns are shown on pages 100–1.

Key to symbols

♂♀ Symbols for male (♂) and female (♀) are used throughout this section.

Key to maps

The maps depict the distribution of quarry species in Britain. These generalised maps show, as far as possible, the normal range of resident species, plus the breeding and main winter distributions of migrant species. Migratory movements and dispersal of some species are quite complex; to avoid over complicating the maps some distributions, such as the influx of Woodpigeons from the Continent or Hooded Crows into eastern England, are omitted. The primary aim is to present a simple guide for the sportsman, to indicate the main distribution of quarry species during the shooting season.

summer   winter

Sedentary and mainly resident species are denoted by dashed lines.

Migratory species, and residents whose populations are supplemented in winter by a significant number of immigrants, are denoted by cross-hatched lines.

Key to shooting season block

The open season is shaded, and dates of opening and closing are specified. All information refers to Britain (England, Scotland and Wales) unless otherwise specified. (Details of shooting seasons, local restrictions, authorisation, etc are given in Chapters 4, 8 and 9.)

Examples:

1. Typical open season for duck: opens 1 September; closes on 31 January inland and 20 February on foreshore.

J	F	M	A	M	J	J	A	S	O	N	D
	31				INLAND				1		
	20				FORESHORE						

2. Woodcock: season opens 1 September (in Scotland), 1 October (England and Wales); closes 31 January (all Britain).

J	F	M	A	M	J	J	A	S	O	N	D
	31				ENGLAND & WALES				1		
					SCOTLAND			1			

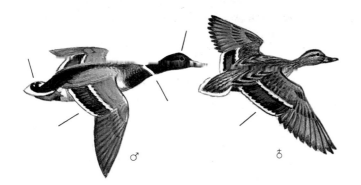

MALLARD

Anas platyrhynchos
size: 58 cm (23 in)

♂   ♂

Large dabbling duck. Adult ♂ characterised by glossy, dark green head, white collar and purple-brown chest; rest of plumage mainly light grey, tail white with black central feathers. ♀ dull, mottled brown. Both sexes have purple speculum bordered by white wing-bars, particularly conspicuous in flight. Juvenile similar to ♀.
Voice: ♀ has characteristic loud, deep *quark* either uttered singly (often in alarm) or several strung together during courtship. ♂ quieter; typical call a soft, nasal *quark* and high whistle.

One of the most widespread of British breeding birds, and the most numerous breeding waterfowl. Frequents a very wide variety of predominantly still, shallow freshwater and brackish wetlands, from small ponds and large reservoirs to marshes, rivers, park lakes and canals. Outside breeding season extends into maritime habitats. Captive-bred birds released on a large scale to supplement wild stock. Breeding population mainly resident; local movements and dispersal of young predominate, although released stock recorded as migrants as far afield as U.S.S.R. Passage migrants and winter visitors include immigrants from Iceland, Scandinavia, northern U.S.S.R. and north-central Europe, but chiefly from Baltic and North Sea countries; normally present September/October to April/May, widespread throughout the country in both coastal and inland areas.

Typically feeds at night, resting by day at safe roost sites. Rises easily and almost vertically from water when flushed; flies quickly with shallow wing-beats. Flies in loose flocks, pairs or singly. Highly gregarious; ♂♂ flock during breeding season, while ♀ incubates; large flocks occur in autumn and winter.
Diet very varied, including wide range of plant and animal material; highly opportunistic feeder. Food obtained from water by sieving and pecking at surface, up-ending, and diving. Usually nests in undergrowth close to water; readily accepts artificial nest structures.

Colouring of ♂ resembles ♂ Red-breasted Merganser (protected). ♀ similar to ♀♀ of other dabbling duck species, particularly Gadwall, Pintail, Shoveler and Wigeon, but both ♂ and ♀ are bigger and more heavily-built than other dabbling ducks.

Field identification

1ˢᵗ. Sept.
31 Jan

Habitat and distribution

Behaviour and feeding

Similar species

J	F	M	A	M	J	J	A	S	O	N	D
	31			INLAND							
	20			FORESHORE		1					

Shooting season

65

TEAL

Anas crecca
size: 36 cm (14 in)

Field identification

1ˢᵗ. Sept.

31 Jan

Habitat and distribution

Behaviour and feeding

Similar species

Very small, compact dabbling duck. ♂ characterised by conspicuous grey plumage contrasting with dark chestnut head, creamy-buff patch on each side of black under-tail coverts and prominent white stripe along scapulars; at close quarters broad green patch extending from in front of eye to nape bordered by narrow buff line is evident; breast cream spotted with black; underside white. Speculum of both sexes green and black, bordered white. ♀ plumage mottled brown with paler cheeks and whitish underside. Juvenile similar to ♀, but more spotted under-parts. *Voice*: ♂ has characteristic low, whistling *crick-crick*; ♀ generally silent, but utters harsh *quack* in alarm.

Breeding birds favour rushy moorland and heathland pools, bogs, etc, typically around small upland waters, but frequently well away from open water; in lowland areas prefers small lakes, rivers, fresh and brackish marshes with good cover. Requires shallow muddy water areas for feeding. In winter and on passage extends to coastal habitats (estuarine flats, salt-marshes, etc) also larger freshwater areas.
British breeding population largely resident, moving south or south-west in autumn. Some emigration from southern England to western Europe and Mediterranean. Large influx of passage migrants and winter immigrants originate from Iceland, Baltic and North Sea countries, Scandinavia and northern U.S.S.R.; main winter concentrations are in south-east England; immigrants appear from the end of August to November, returning March to early May.

Extremely agile in flight, frequently in tight packs; rises vertically from water or land and flies fast with characteristic very rapid wing-beats; long distance flights normally high, in lines or V-formation. Gregarious outside breeding season, often in small flocks; more dispersed in small parties, pairs or singly while feeding. Feeds primarily at night, often moving several miles from safe day-time roost to feeding area. Food obtained by dabbling in shallow, muddy water. Diet varies according to season and locality; seeds predominate in autumn and winter; increasing amount of animal material taken in summer.
Nests in thick cover on ground, normally close to water.

Only species of similar size is Garganey (protected) – a summer visitor.

	J	F	M	A	M	J	J	A	S	O	N	D
INLAND		31										
FORESHORE		20							1				

Shooting season

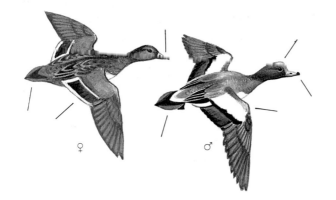

WIGEON

Anas penelope
size: 46 cm (18 in)

Medium-sized, short-necked dabbling duck. Basic plumage colour of ♂ is grey, with buff forehead and crown and remainder of head chestnut; chest pinkish-brown, white under-parts; characteristic white shoulder patch readily seen in flight. ♀ duller; brown plumage tinged rufous, white underside, green speculum fringed with white wing-bars. Short bill and dark pointed tail useful diagnostic characters.
Voice: highly distinctive whistling *whee oo* of ♂, typically heard from flocks in flight; ♀♀ virtually silent.

Field identification

1ˢᵗ. Sept.
31 Jan.

Small British breeding population restricted to upland lochs, pools and streams in open moorland, bogs and wooded country. Chiefly maritime outside breeding season, mainly on mud-flats and saltings; recently taken to inland flood-meadows especially in eastern England.
British population mostly resident, moving to coast in autumn with some south-westerly movements to Ireland. Passage migrants and winter immigrants, chiefly from Iceland, Scandinavia and northern U.S.S.R., mainly present September to April. Occurs in large numbers, particularly in east and south-east England, south-west and north-east Scotland.

Habitat and distribution

Highly gregarious outside breeding season. Very large feeding flocks occur; often roosts in large numbers on sea, sand-flats, etc. Usually roosts during day, feeding at night, but may reverse pattern depending on prevailing tidal and weather conditions. Grazes predominantly on grasses, usually while walking over exposed vegetation, but frequently feeds from water surface. Takes mainly leaves, stems, roots, etc of grasses and herbs, seeds and some animal material.
Nests on ground in heather, bracken or rank grasses.

Behaviour and feeding

♀ resembles other ♀ dabbling ducks, especially Shoveler, Pintail, Gadwall and Mallard.

Similar species

J	F	M	A	M	J	J	A	S	O	N	D
	31			INLAND							
	20			FORESHORE		1					

Shooting season

PINTAIL

Anas acuta
size: 56 cm (22 in)

♀   ♂

Field identification

1ˢᵗ· Seþt·

31 Jan

Habitat and distribution

Behaviour and feeding

Similar species

Large, slim-built dabbling duck with noticeably long neck and extended central pair of tail feathers forming characteristic needle-tail of ♂, and shorter but still pointed tail of ♀. ♂ has dark brown head, and back of neck, contrasting with pure white breast, sides and front of neck, extending as white streak up side of head; under-parts white; back and flanks light grey; rump black; wings grey and brown with green speculum conspicuous in flight. ♀ duller, with grey-brown plumage and no discernible wing-pattern in flight, except a light trailing edge to inner wing. Juvenile resembles ♀, but generally darker and more uniform.
Voice: generally silent; ♂ has low Teal-like whistle, ♀ has a hoarse *quack*.

Small British breeding population widely distributed in a diverse range of habitats, including moorland pools, freshwater marshes and damp, rough grassland in low-lying areas.
In winter chiefly a coastal species, found mainly in estuarine and other sheltered coastal areas; also on inland flood-lands and freshwater marshes, and sometimes agricultural land.
Mainly migratory; British breeding birds move south, but possibly remain within Britain; augmented in autumn by passage migrants and winter visitors from Iceland, Scandinavia and north-western U.S.S.R. Immigrants appear in mid-September, departing in April.

Highly gregarious outside breeding season; flocks vary in size from small parties to several thousands on larger waters. Typically feeds at night and remains relatively inactive during daylight. Swims high on water; feeds mainly by up-ending or dabbling. Flight is fast and direct with rapid wing-beats; often fly in long lines or V-formation.
Diet includes a wide variety of plant and animal material, chiefly from bottom mud in shallow water. Will also feed on stubble grain or dig plant roots and underground stems.
Nests on ground usually in short cover; often in loose colonies; primarily on islands in lakes and adjacent to moorland pools.

Although ♂ readily distinguished, ♀ resembles other ♀ dabbling ducks, particularly Mallard, Gadwall, Shoveler and Wigeon.

J	F	M	A	M	J	J	A	S	O	N	D
	31				INLAND						
	20				FORESHORE		1				

Shooting season

68

SHOVELER

Anas clypeata
size: 51 cm (20 in)

Medium-sized dabbling duck; both sexes characterised by enormous spatulate bill, large head and short neck, which are readily discernible both in flight and on the water. ♂ has striking pattern of dark green head, chestnut flanks and belly contrasting with pure white chest, which is noticeable at considerable distances; pale blue forewing, green speculum edged with white, ♀ primarily mottled brown, with similar but duller blue forewing and green speculum. Juvenile a dull version of ♀
Voice: generally silent outside breeding season.

Breeding population thinly but widely distributed; main concentration in southern and eastern England. Restricted chiefly to shallow, nutrient-rich fresh and brackish waters throughout the year. British birds migrate south to France, Spain and into Africa; large numbers pass through Britain on migration; smaller numbers overwinter. Immigrants and passage migrants originate from Iceland, Scandinavia and U.S.S.R. Local birds normally leave by late October; main passage through Britain occurs in November; main return movements March/April.

Characteristic appearance when swimming, with front end carried low and huge bill angled down. Feeds primarily by swimming with head and neck submerged and surface feeding, moving head from side-to-side filtering out food particles; occasionally up-ends. Diet varied, including microscopic animals, seeds and other plant material. Predominately a day-time feeder usually singly, in pairs or small flocks. Flight agile with rapid wing-beats; makes loud whistling noise in flight; wings appear set well-back on body; rises easily from water with characteristic drumming sound. Particularly active on the wing in April.
Nests usually close to water, on ground in variety of habitats from rushes to open, short grassland and low scrub.

Huge bill distinctive, but plumage of ♀ similar to that of ♀ Gadwall, Pintail, Mallard and Wigeon.

Field identification

1st. SEPT.
31 JAN.

Habitat and distribution

Behaviour and feeding

Similar species

J	F	M	A	M	J	J	A	S	O	N	D
	31				INLAND						
	20				FORESHORE		1				

Shooting season

GADWALL

Anas strepera
size: 51 cm (20 in)

Field identification

1ˢᵗ Sept.

31 Jan

Habitat and distribution

Behaviour and feeding

Similar species

Medium-sized dabbling duck. ♂ has uniform grey-brown plumage and conspicuous black rump; distinctive white speculum forms a bold white patch on trailing edge of wing, readily seen in flight; wing coverts chestnut and black. ♀ dull, mottled brown, with white belly and white wing-patch as ♂. Juvenile much like ♀, but well marked with streaks and spots on underside and darker upper-parts.
Voice: ♀ has high-pitched *quack*; ♂ has a short nasal call.

Prefers shallow, nutrient-rich, sheltered lakes, slow-moving streams, and freshwater marshes of lowland Britain; outside breeding season also found on brackish and saline waters. Establishment in Britain as a breeding species aided by escapes from collections and release of captive-bred birds. English population mainly resident, but Scottish birds move southwards to England and Ireland and some movement of birds from East Anglia to western Europe and Mediterranean. Winter visitors chiefly from Iceland, Baltic and North Sea countries; arrive mainly October/November, returning March/April.

Tends to be fairly secretive and retiring throughout year; rarely gathers in large flocks; frequently mixes in small numbers with other dabbling ducks. Swims high in water; very mobile on both land and water, as well as in air. Flies with rapid beats of apparently pointed wings, producing whistling sound in flight. Normally a day-time feeder; may spend much time flying between roost and feeding sites. Feeds mainly on aquatic plant material, obtained either by swimming with head under water or dabbling; also steals food from other waterbirds; will occasionally feed on land, grazing and taking grain from stubble fields.
Nests on ground, close to water in very dense vegetation.

Size close to that of Mallard; ♀ plumage resembles ♀ Mallard, Pintail, Wigeon and Shoveler.

	J	F	M	A	M	J	J	A	S	O	N	D
		31				INLAND						
		20				FORESHORE			1			

Shooting season

TUFTED DUCK
Aythya fuligula
size: 43 cm (17 in)

Small diving duck. Adult ♂ black with white flanks and belly; long, thin, drooping crest. ♀ rich dark brown head and back; flanks and underside paler; crest shorter than in adult ♂. In flight both sexes appear black with white belly and a distinctive broad white wing-bar. Juvenile resembles ♀.
Voice: virtually silent except during courtship.

Field identification

1ˢᵗ· ꟻᴇᴘᴛ.

31 JAN

Frequents open fresh waters of all sizes. During breeding season prefers more secluded, small- to moderate-sized lakes, particularly with fringing reeds or similar cover and vegetated islands. In winter readily takes to larger open waters such as reservoirs. Rarely found on sea. Widespread breeding species throughout lowland areas of British Isles. Marked range extension and population increase in recent decades; readily colonises new breeding habitats created by gravel excavation, etc. In winter local populations show some southerly movement within the country. British population augmented by birds from Iceland, northern and western Europe. Immigrants usually arrive mid-September/mid-November, depart late February/mid-May, and are found throughout the country, with notable concentrations on reservoirs in south and east England.

Habitat and distribution

Behaviour and feeding

Frequently uses same water area for both feeding and roosting, thus avoiding need to flight to and from feeding sites. Feeds mainly morning and evening. Normally shifts position if disturbed before flighting off water. Patters for some distance on take-off; flight usually straight and rapid, with quick beats of short wings. Dives in generally shallow waters; food mainly animal material, supplemented by vegetation (grasses, duckweed, etc).
Nests typically close to water in bushes or rushes; occasionally found in loose colonies, especially on islands.

♂ resembles ♂ Scaup (protected); ♀ similar to ♀ Pochard and Scaup (protected).

Similar species

J	F	M	A	M	J	J	A	S	O	N	D
	31				INLAND						
	20				FORESHORE			1			

Shooting season

71

POCHARD

Aythya ferina
size: 46 cm (18 in)

♂   ♀

Field identification

1ˢᵗ. Sept.
31 Jan

Habitat and distribution

Behaviour and feeding

Similar species

Shooting season

Medium-sized diving duck with 'dumpy' appearance on water. ♂ has dark chestnut head and neck contrasting with pale grey back and flanks, black breast and tail. ♀ uniform dull brown, slightly paler around face. Both sexes characterised in flight by absence of white on wings; pale grey wing-bar runs full length of wing, forewing dark grey. Juvenile resembles ♀.
Voice: virtually silent except during courtship.

Sparse British breeding population favours larger lowland lakes, sluggish streams, etc, with dense fringing vegetation, and preferably islands. Found on larger freshwater areas, such as reservoirs, in winter; rarely in brackish or maritime habitats. Most British birds resident, but move away from breeding areas in winter; some emigrate to west Europe and Mediterranean. Passage migrants and winter visitors occur mainly during October to April; widely distributed, but with large concentrations in central lowlands of Scotland, central and southern England.

Gregarious outside breeding season, normally in small parties, occasionally flocks of several thousands. Spends most of time on water; take-off from water laboured, but when airborne has strong, fast flight with rapid beats of short wings making whistling sound. Flocks normally fly in tight group; long distance flights in lines or V-formation. Rarely occurs on land. Roosts during day in flocks on open water; feeds chiefly after dark in evening and early morning, less actively in middle of night. Diet mainly vegetable matter, including seeds, stems, leaves, etc, obtained normally by diving, occasionally by up-ending in shallower water; some animal material taken.
Nests on ground, normally in thick cover close to water; frequently by or on water, elevated above surface on rush or reed base.

♂ readily distinguished; ♀ resembles ♀ Tufted Duck and Scaup (protected).

J	F	M	A	M	J	J	A	S	O	N	D
	31			INLAND							
	20			FORESHORE			1				

72

GOLDENEYE

Bucephala clangula
size: 46 cm (18 in)

Medium-sized diving duck. ♂ has high-crowned, dark head with greenish-purple gloss and circular white patch on cheek; neck and under-parts white contrasting with black back and rump and grey tail; extensive white on inner wing readily seen in flight. ♀ smaller than ♂; has chocolate-brown head, pale blue-grey upper-parts with white under-parts, grey flanks and tail; wings dark with conspicuous white patch similar to ♂. Juvenile closely resembles ♀.
Voice: generally silent, except during courtship display.

Breeding habitat is tall forests close to moderately deep, productive open waters. During passage and on migration will make use of a variety of open water – lakes, reservoirs, streams, estuaries, etc. Migratory, but small British breeding population possibly undertakes only local movements; immigrants, mainly from Scandinavia, arrive from mid-September and return March/early May.

Gregarious outside breeding season, normally in small flocks; spends most time on water or in flight, rarely comes to land. Mainly diurnal feeder; roost frequently considerable distance from feeding area. Flies with rapid wing-beats creating a characteristic loud whistling. Feeds chiefly on animal material, especially molluscs, crustaceans and insect larvae, obtained by diving to middle depths or bottom of feeding water. Nests in holes in trees; readily takes to nest boxes.

Both sexes readily distinguished from other diving-duck species.

Field identification

1ˢᵗ· Sept.
31 Jan.

Habitat and distribution

Behaviour and feeding

Similar species

J	F	M	A	M	J	J	A	S	O	N	D	
	31			INLAND								
	20			FORESHORE			1					

Shooting season

73

GREYLAG GOOSE

Anser anser
size: 75–90 cm (30–35 in)

Field identification

The largest grey goose. Head, neck and most of body uniform pale brownish-grey. Characterised by large size, heavy head and neck with stout bill, and very pale blueish-grey forewing – the latter especially obvious in flight. Bill bright orange with no black, and a white nail, legs flesh-pink. Breast often spotted with black. Young birds similar to adults, but generally unspotted, with greyer legs.
Voice: like domestic goose; a deep, loud nasal call; flight call loud, characteristically a deep cackle.

In summer grazes in a variety of wetland habitats from lakes and marshes, agricultural pasture, to upland bogs and moorland. British breeding birds mostly resident. In autumn and winter immigrants generally found on agricultural pasture and cultivated land, marshes and estuaries. Some local movements of breeding populations occur; main influx of Icelandic breeding birds occurs in late October, and departure is generally mid-April. Highest concentration of immigrants is found in east-central Scotland.

Habitat and distribution

Behaviour and feeding

Flight rapid and powerful, with regular beats of broad wings; characteristic circular flutter of wings on landing; takes off with ease from ground, although with more difficulty from water.
Usually flights from roosts to feeding grounds in early morning. Gregarious outside breeding season. Largest flocks usually occur in autumn when feeding on stubble and potato fields. Often found in mixed flocks with Pink-footed Geese where winter ranges overlap. Feeds almost entirely on plant material, normally grazing on land, but will feed on water, up-ending for submerged material. In autumn and winter normally feeds on grassland, cereal root crops, etc; late spring diet includes growing cereals.
Nests on ground either amongst heather (Scottish moors and bogs) or in bushes, reedbeds or other dense vegetation providing shelter; especially on islands; often colonial and rarely far from water.

Similar species

Can be confused with Bean (protected), Pink-footed and White-fronted Geese (especially immature birds), but all are smaller and more slightly built by comparison; calls are also distinctive.

J	F	M	A	M	J	J	A	S	O	N	D
	31			INLAND						1	
	20			FORESHORE							

Shooting season

74

PINK-FOOTED GOOSE

Anser brachyrhynchus
size: 60–76 cm (24–30 in)

Field identification

Medium-sized, grey goose characterised by dark head and neck, contrasting with pale brownish body. Bill is small and short, dark coloured with a pink band; feet and legs are pink. Back and wings grey; paler forewing noticeable in flight. Young birds darker and more uniform above, mottled appearance below compared with more uniform colouring of adults.
Voice: characteristic short, high-pitched flight notes; also lower, more musical nasal calls.

Breeding range in Arctic, from east Greenland and Iceland to Spitzbergen. Birds visiting Britain originate from Iceland and Greenland, nesting in coastal area of north-east Greenland and south-central Iceland. Winters in northern Britain and Ireland, with main concentrations in eastern Scotland. Arrives in September/October and departs April or early May. Found mainly on arable land, roosting on sand- and mud-flats in estuaries, inland lochs or reservoirs in moorland adjoining feeding areas.

Habitat and distribution

Autumn and winter flocks may comprise several thousand birds. Tend to feed by day but occasionally (especially under full moon) will stay out well into night or flight out to feed by night and roost during the day. Roost sites may be several miles from feeding area. During autumn feed mainly on barley stubble and potatoes. Pastures used throughout winter, and in spring feeds exclusively on grass and winter cereals; carrots and brassicas are taken in some districts.

Behaviour and feeding

Can be confused with Greylag, Bean (protected) and White-fronted Geese (especially immature birds); voices are characteristic.

Similar species

J	F	M	A	M	J	J	A	S	O	N	D
	31				INLAND						
	20				FORESHORE		1				

Shooting season

75

WHITE-FRONTED GOOSE

Anser albifrons
size: 66–76 cm (26–30 in)

Two races of the White-fronted Goose regularly occur in the British Isles, the European White-front (*Anser a. albifrons*) and Greenland White-front (*A. a. flavirostris*). The two sub-species are distinguishable in the field and have markedly different winter ranges (see distribution map). The following description relates to the European White-front, as current legislation does not provide for an open season for White-fronts in Scotland where the majority of the Greenland sub-species occur.

Field identification

Greenland population

European population

Habitat and distribution

Medium-sized grey goose characterised by white band at base of upper bill and black barring on belly. Amount of black on underside extremely variable. Young birds lack these characters, but are normally found in the company of adults. Generally dark greyish-brown plumage, fairly long, pink bill, orange legs.
Voice: generally noisy species; typically high-pitched, musical cackle; flight call normally two or three syllable, short metallic notes.

Breeding range in northern Siberia, within the Arctic Circle. Western section of population winters in Baltic and North Sea countries. Winter haunts in Britain located in south and east-central Wales and in southern England (Greenland White-front occurs in Scotland, Ireland and a few localities in west-central Wales). Arrives during October to January; departs March/April. Found mainly in lowland wet grasslands and marshes, arable fields, etc.

Behaviour and feeding

Normally feeds during day, usually close to roost and in undisturbed conditions will roost on feeding area. Congregate on arable land in autumn, feeding primarily on grass and stubble grain. Other food recorded includes potatoes, weed seeds, and clover. Flight noticeably more easy than other grey geese; quicker and more agile on the wing, and can take off almost vertically when disturbed. Large flocks gather on migration, but tends to split more readily into family parties and smaller groups than other grey geese.

Similar species

Can be confused with Greylag, Bean (protected) and Pink-footed Geese (especially immature birds), but generally distinguished by small size, uniformly dark plumage, and distinctive 'musical' call notes.

Shooting season
ENGLAND & WALES ONLY:
PROTECTED IN SCOTLAND

J	F	M	A	M	J	J	A	S	O	N	D
	31				INLAND						
	20				FORESHORE			1			

CANADA GOOSE

Branta canadensis
Size: 91–102 cm (36–40 in)

Very large grey-brown goose; black head and neck with distinctive white patch extending from the chin across cheeks to behind the eye. Body dark above; paler brown flanks and under-parts; tail-coverts white, tail black. Bill and legs black. Young birds similar to adult, and generally indistinguishable in field.
Voice: considerable variety of calls, but flight note is characteristically a deep, loud, resonant, trumpeting honk.

Field identification

Introduced to England from North America in 17th century. Feral population generally resident, but local movements occur outside breeding season, and moult-migration to Scotland has evolved in Yorkshire sub-population since 1950s. Found in variety of lowland wetland habitats from ornamental park lakes (where first established) to freshwater marshes, gravel pits, etc; frequently close to human habitation.

Habitat and distribution

Feeds mostly during day; grass is prime constituent of diet throughout the year, supplemented by some insect matter in summer. Will also take clover and cereals; and sometimes up-end in water to feed on submerged vegetation. Gregarious, especially outside breeding season. Flight fast, with deep, regular wing-beats; often flies at low levels. Frequently walks from roost site to feeding area.
Usually nests on ground; prefers islands in open waters or marshes. Nest is normally under bushes or other sheltered spot. Frequently colonial, but pairs highly territorial and aggressive.

Behaviour and feeding

Not easily confused with other species of geese. The largest European goose: much larger than Brent and Barnacle (both protected), with characteristic black and white pattern on head and neck.

Similar species

J	F	M	A	M	J	J	A	S	O	N	D
	31			INLAND							
	20			FORESHORE			1				

Shooting season

77

MOORHEN
Gallinula chloropus
size: 33 cm (13 in)

Field identification

Small-sized, dark waterbird. Striking white flank stripes and under-tail coverts contrast with dark brownish to black upper-parts and slate-grey under-parts. Bill and frontal shield bright red; yellow bill tip. Sexes similar; juveniles brownish with creamy flank stripes, white under-tail coverts and greenish-brown bill.
Voice: loud call notes include a sharp metallic *krick*.

Breeding habitats include a wide variety of freshwater environments throughout most of the country; particularly in smaller ponds, ditches, sluggish streams, etc, but also in reed-beds, damp meadows, and larger lakes often in towns and cities. Frequently feeds away from water in adjacent grassland, etc. Found on larger waters outside breeding season. Most British birds resident, but local movements occur; some immigrants from western Europe occur mainly in eastern England

Habitat and distribution during autumn and winter.

Behaviour and feeding

Solitary, in pairs or small parties; may gather into larger flocks during winter. Swims with jerky head action and tail cocked; flicks tail when anxious. Quite reluctant to fly, often seeking cover when disturbed; takes off from water by pattering along surface; flies low and fast with rapid wing-beats and trailing legs. May roost in trees and bushes. Feeds in water, pulling plant material, etc from surface, or walking through damp grassland. Diet varied; includes leaves, grass, seeds and fruit, also insects, eggs, earthworms, slugs, small fish, etc.
Nest usually in aquatic vegetation cover at waterside or close to water in adjacent undergrowth; normally constructed of dead reeds, sedge, etc.

Similar species

Only likely to be confused with Coot.

Shooting season

COOT
Fulica atra
size: 38 cm (15 in)

Medium-sized bulky waterbird, characterised by overall very dark slate-grey body colour and black head in sharp contrast to white bill and frontal shield. On water distinguished by rounded back and apparently small head. Sexes similar; juvenile dark brown above, pale brown and whitish under-parts.
Voice: call a loud, sharp *kowk*.

Field identification

Inhabits mainly lowland open waters and slow-flowing streams. Normally requires minimum of a half hectare (one acre) of open water for breeding territory. Prefers shallow, nutrient-rich waters. Very large flocks occur in winter on reservoirs and other large expanses of open water, especially in southern England. British breeding population largely resident, with some movement away from higher altitudes and northern areas outside breeding season. European birds overwinter in large numbers, mainly in eastern and southern England.

Habitat and distribution

Highly territorial and aggressive in breeding season; gregarious at other times, winter flocks often congregating into large rafts. Swims and dives easily; normally reluctant to fly, but when forced to do so takes off from water by pattering along the surface in the manner of diving ducks. Flight normally low and ungainly with neck and legs extended; generally only flies for short distances. Obtains food mainly by diving to collect plant material from middle or lower depths; dives prolonged and food brought to surface to be consumed. In winter will also graze on damp grassland areas close to open water. Diet mainly leaves, stems, etc. of aquatic plants, also some animal material.
Nest normally among aquatic vegetation fringing open water; constructed of dead leaves from tall marsh plants.

Behaviour and feeding

Only likely to be confused with Moorhen; frequently associates with diving ducks, but readily distinguished from these.

Similar species

J	F	M	A	M	J	J	A	S	O	N	D
	31						1				

Shooting season

GOLDEN PLOVER

Pluvialis apricaria
size: 28 cm (11 in)

WINTER PLUMAGE

Field identification

1ˢᵗ Sept.

31 Jan ˢᵗ

Habitat and distribution

Behaviour and feeding

Similar species

Medium-sized wader with short, straight bill and rounded head. Distinguished at all seasons by rich gold and black spotted plumage on back and wings, white under-wing, and dark tail; no wing-bar. Face and under-parts in summer black with yellowish-white fringing stripe from forehead and neck to flanks. In winter underside and face whitish, mottled gold-brown. Juveniles more uniform than adults, paler above and darker below.
Voice: call note and characteristic clear, liquid *tlui* uttered in alarm, and normally in flight.

Breeding birds typically haunt flat or gently undulating moorlands, upland grass-heaths and peat bogs. Move from hills in winter to lowland farmland and coastal habitats, occurring on arable and pasture farmland, estuaries, etc. British population largely resident, moving to lowlands and coasts; supplemented by passage migrants and winter visitors mainly from Iceland and Scandinavia, during September to April or May.

Gregarious outside breeding season; normally found in flocks, frequently in association with Lapwings (protected) on inland roosts and feeding sites. Flock flies in compact group; flight rapid and very agile. On ground has upright stance when still; walks with rapid steps tilting to gather food items. Diet varied; mainly insects, worms, crustaceans, seeds, berries, etc.
Nests on ground in short heather or grass heath.

Confusion most likely with Grey Plover (protected), which is a winter visitor to coastal areas of Britain.

Shooting season

J	F	M	A	M	J	J	A	S	O	N	D
	31						1				

SNIPE

Gallinago gallinago
size: 27 cm (10½ in)

Small, brown wader with characteristic long, straight bill. Upper-parts rufous brown and black with golden-buff stripes on head and back; under-parts buff with dark brown markings and pale barred flanks. Juvenile resembles adult.
Voice: when flushed normally utters sharp, grating call note.

Field identification

Breeding habitat is typically wet grassland, bogs, marshes, etc, occasionally drier moorland sites. In winter frequents a wide variety of wetlands, including freshwater and salt-marshes, usually in lowland areas. Breeding birds largely resident, undergoing local movements mainly to lower ground, with some emigration to western Europe. Passage migrants and winter visitors occur, frequently in large numbers, during September to April, originating chiefly from Iceland, Scandinavia, Baltic states and western U.S.S.R.

Habitat and distribution

Generally secretive. Normally rests during day in rank vegetation, feeding most actively at dusk. In winter feeds more freely in open and during daylight. Small flocks may gather outside breeding season in feeding areas. Crouches when disturbed, often rising only when closely approached; characteristic zig-zag flight when flushed, frequently drops down to cover rapidly from considerable height. Food chiefly animal matter, including worms, molluscs and insects.
Nests on ground in tussock of grass or rushes, occasionally amongst heather.

Behaviour and feeding

Most easily confused with Jack Snipe (protected), which is much smaller and characteristically rises silently, very reluctantly (normally at walker's feet) and pitches down into cover after short flight. Woodcock somewhat similar to Snipe, but larger with stouter bill and heavier build.

Similar species

J	F	M	A	M	J	J	A	S	O	N	D
	31					12					

Shooting season

WOODCOCK
Scolopax rusticola
size: 34 cm (13½ in)

Field identification

1ˢᵗ. Nov.

31 Jan

Medium-sized, dark, round-winged wader with long straight bill. Plumage richly marked with browns, buff and black on upper-parts; under-parts light brown with fine dark-brown barring. Exceptionally well-camouflaged while at rest in woodland; in flight looks stout with short tail and long bill angled downwards. Sexes similar; young resemble adults.
Voice: virtually silent except during roding flights in spring and early summer.

Habitat and distribution

Essentially a forest wader; breeding habitat typically dry, deciduous woodland with open, damp grassland areas for feeding; also in mixed broad-leaved and coniferous woodland and forestry plantations in northern parts of range. In winter retains affinity for woodland cover and open areas to feed. British breeding population largely sedentary, with some local movements. Autumn migrants from Scandinavia, Baltic states and western U.S.S.R. normally arrive in Britain mid-October to mid-November, overwintering mainly in western and southern districts; return migration mainly March to mid-April.

Behaviour and feeding

Solitary and secretive. Rests during day in woodland ground vegetation. Flushed birds fly rapidly, dodging and weaving, and dropping quickly to cover again; rise with distinctive 'swish' of wings. Crepuscular, making regular flights to feeding grounds at dusk; also feeds in daylight in adverse weather conditions. Diet mainly animal material; earthworms of particular importance, also insects and larvae; uses long bill to probe deeply into soft ground to extract food.
Nests within woodland, often by trunk of tree or fallen branch, frequently in more open areas amongst bracken or brambles.

Similar species

Distinguished from Snipe by larger size, heavy appearance, thick bill, and to some extent by habitat preferences.

Shooting season

PHEASANT

Phasianus colchicus
size: ♂ 76–89 cm (30–35 in)
     ♀ 53–64 cm (21–25 in)

Large gamebird; both sexes characterised by long, pointed tail. ♂ colouring very variable, but typically iridescent copper body plumage with glossy dark green head, scarlet wattle and white neck ring. ♀ about 30 per cent smaller than ♂, duller, mottled plumage tones varying from light buff to dark brown. Juvenile similar to adult ♀.
Voice: ♂ has a characteristic harsh, resonant crowing call; ♀ less vocal, but utters soft whistle when flushed.

Field identification

Mainly a lowland bird favouring wooded agricultural land, parkland, etc; wild population also frequents more open habitats, particularly marshes and occasionally moorland. Resident; extensively released into areas managed specifically for the benefit of this species.

Habitat and distribution

Very conspicuous, feeding in open, often in wet pastures and cultivated land adjacent to woodland. Tends to avoid flying unless forced; noisy take-off and strong flight with whirring wing-beats, flight usually direct and rapid but seldom sustained; will fly hard and fast for short period, then glide towards cover. Gregarious, often gather in flocks to feed; sexes frequently segregated. Normally roosts in trees; also takes to trees to avoid danger. Feeds on wide variety of plant and animal matter including seeds, fruits, green shoots, leaves, insects, earthworms, slugs, etc.
Ground-nesting usually in dense cover of tall grass, hedgerow, scrub, etc.

Behaviour and feeding

Large size and long tail are unmistakable characteristics; a wide range of colour variants occur; confusion can occur with feral birds of introduced species, particularly Golden and Lady Amherst's Pheasants.

Similar species

J	F	M	A	M	J	J	A	S	O	N	D
	1							1			

Shooting season

83

GREY PARTRIDGE

Perdix perdix
size: ♂ 31 cm (12 in)
　　　♀ 29 cm (11½ in)

♂　　　♂

Field identification

1ˢᵗ. Nov.
15ᵀᴴ Nos .

Small, rotund gamebird with short wings and short, rufous tail. Sexes essentially similar, although ♂ slightly larger; both have characteristic orange-chestnut face, grey neck and under-parts and chestnut flanks; ♂ has conspicuous dark chestnut horse-shoe patch on lower breast, but this feature usually only poorly developed in ♀. Juvenile has orange or chestnut markings replaced by brown streaking.
Voice: usual call a loud, high-pitched, grating *kirr-ic*.

Habitat and distribution

Found principally in mixed farmland areas preferring extensive tracts of grassland with fringing hedgerows, rough grass or woodland cover, and some open ground. Mainly restricted to lowlands, but does occur up to 600 m (2000 ft) on moors and grass heaths adjacent to cultivated land. Frequently occurs in sand dunes, marshes and bogs.
Resident, with some local dispersal in autumn and winter months.

Behaviour and feeding

Almost exclusively ground-dwelling; normally walks or runs with rounded back and head low, but runs for cover with neck stretched up. Often crouches when alarmed; flies reluctantly, but when flushed flight strong and rapid with groups keeping well together.
Gregarious outside breeding season; with flock structure retained from early August to late winter. Pairs strongly territorial in breeding season. Feeds largely on plant material; ♀♀ feeding young also take insects. Main components of diet are grass, leaves, cereals and clover, grain and other plant seeds.
Nests on ground in hedgerows, scrub or rough grassland; also in arable crops and cultivated grassland.

Similar species

Easily confused with slightly larger Red-legged Partridge; in particular, juveniles of the two species are very similar and difficult to separate. Quail (protected) is similar, but much smaller.

Shooting season

| J | F | M | A | M | J | J | A | S | O | N | D |

84

RED-LEGGED PARTRIDGE

Alectoris rufa
size: ♂ 34 cm (13½ in)
 ♀ 32 cm (13 in)

Small, rotund gamebird with short wings and tail. Sexes have similar plumage, but ♂ slightly larger than ♀. Adult has distinctive long white eye-stripe, white throat and cheeks bordered black; chestnut, white and black barred flanks; red bill and legs; rest of plumage olive brown, grey and buff. Juvenile lacks distinctive head pattern and barred flanks.
Voice: call-note of ♂ a low, harsh *chucka chucka*; both sexes utter sharp, barking *kuk-kuk* when flushed.

1ˢᵗ. Nov. ♀
15ᵗʰ Nov. ♂

Prefers dry, lowland areas, especially sandy heaths, chalk downs and open fields on light soils with low vegetation; occurs in a variety of habitats from open woodland to arable fields and pasture.
Introduced species; resident and largely sedentary.
Frequently released, and on an increasing scale in recent years.

Habitat and distribution

Normally walks or runs quickly over open terrain; may roost in trees as well as on ground. Flies very reluctantly, and coveys inclined to scatter when flushed from cover; flight typical of gamebird species. Gregarious outside breeding season; frequently in large flocks (over 50 birds). Solitary and in pairs during breeding period. Feeds largely on plant material – particularly grain, weed seeds, leaves, also roots (e.g. of sugar beet) and legumes; insects taken in late spring.
Nests on ground, usually sheltered by tussock of vegetation, bush, rocks, etc.

Behaviour and feeding

Easily confused with Grey Partridge, especially in flight. Quail (protected) is very much smaller, with duller plumage.

Similar species

J F M A M J J A S O N D

Shooting season

85

RED GROUSE

Lagopus lagopus scoticus
size: ♂ 36–39 cm (14–15½ in)
♀ 33–36 cm (13–14 in)

1ˢᵗ. Sept.
30ᵗʰ. Sept.

Field identification

Medium sized grouse characterised by rotund appearance, short wings; body plumage uniform dark rufous brown with darker wings and black rounded tail. Sexes closely similar, but ♀ more barred and a duller rufous colour. Adults appear greyer in winter, with white under-wing coverts and occasionally show white on flanks and belly. Juvenile generally like ♀.
Voice: call when flushed a loud, crowing *kok*.

Primarily associated with open upland moorland and bogs dominated by heather; also in grass heaths with heather or other dwarf shrubs. Highest densities occur on well-managed heather moor on rich soils, giving optimum supply of food and shelter, mainly in eastern parts of range; poorer soils and preponderance of wet grassy heaths in west result in lower numbers. Resident, moves to lower ground and occasionally cultivated land in winter.

Habitat and distribution

Behaviour and feeding

Basically a ground-dwelling bird, flies for short distances, usually close to ground unless driven higher. Flight strong and rapid, alternating between whirring wing-beats and gliding on decurved wings. Mainly gregarious outside breeding season; packs develop in early autumn as family parties disperse; normally up to 20 in a flock, occasionally more. ♂♂ become strongly territorial as winter progresses; non-territorial ♂♂ and ♀♀ remain in packs. Feeds almost exclusively on heather – particularly young shoots – throughout the year, but will take other plant material; insects may form a significant part of adult diet on blanket bogs and heather moors, and also taken by chicks at an early age.

Similar species

May be confused with ♀ Black Grouse; Ptarmigan always recognisable by smaller size and white wings and underparts.

	J	F	M	A	M	J	J	A	S	O	N	D
Shooting season								12			10	

BLACK GROUSE

Lyrurus tetrix (Tetrao tetrix)
size: ♂ 53 cm (21 in)
♀ 41 13 cm (16–17 in)

LEK DISPLAY POSTURE

Field identification

Medium-sized grouse. Sexes dissimilar. ♂ (Blackcock) plumage glossy blue-black with white wing-bar and curled, 'lyre-shaped' outer-tail feathers. ♀ (Greyhen) warm brown above, greyer and paler under-parts, mottled and barred with black throughout; forked tail. ♂ in eclipse plumage during autumn looks dingy, without characteristic lyre-shaped tail. Juveniles like small dull ♀.
Voice: ♂ usually silent away from lek; ♀ call-note a loud *tchuk*.

Prefers margins of hilly moors, adjacent to woodlands (including conifer plantations), marshes, bogs, etc. Typical habitat includes scattered groups of trees with good cover, and clearings for display grounds. Resident; ♂ particularly sedentary; ♀♀ and juveniles seldom move great distances.

Habitat and distribution

Flight strong and rapid, usually over short distances only; frequently higher than other moorland gamebirds, but low in cover; often circles both on take-off and landing. Gregarious throughout the year, especially ♂♂; large winter flocks can occur. Perches in trees, feeds in trees in winter; roosts and feeds on ground in summer. Feeds chiefly on plant material throughout year; summer diet includes leaves and shoots of ground plants, seeds, berries, fruits, etc, and some insects. Autumn and winter food primarily shoots and buds of birch and Scots pine.
Nests on ground in dense vegetation.

Behaviour and feeding

♂ unmistakable, but ♀ may be confused with ♀ Red Grouse or Capercaillie. Confusing hybrids between Black Grouse and Capercaillie, Red Grouse and Pheasant occur.

Similar species

| J | F | M | A | M | J | J | A | S | O | N | D |

Shooting season

87

PTARMIGAN

Lagopus mutus
size: 33–36 cm (13–14 in)

SUMMER PLUMAGE   SUMMER PLUMAGE   WINTER PLUMAGE

Field identification

Small grouse; both ♂ and ♀ characterised by pure white wings and under-parts at all seasons. Three distinct seasonal plumage variations. In winter both sexes pure white except for black tail. ♂ in summer has dark greyish-brown and black mottled head, neck, flanks, upper breast and upper body and black tail; ♀ browner with tawny markings. ♂ in autumn replaces dark plumage with paler colours, tail remains black; ♀ darker. Juvenile like autumn ♀, but with pale brown wings and tail same colour as back.
Voice: call notes a low, grating croak and repeated cackling, often as alarm.

Habitat and distribution

Resident, restricted to arctic-alpine heaths. In summer found on high-level, open rocky or stony terrain with abundant bilberry and cranberry; generally above 600 m (2000 ft) in Cairngorms, at lower elevations further north; moves to lower ground in winter.

Behaviour and feeding

Frequently tame and easily approached; flies reluctantly, preferring to crouch and skulk, relying on immaculate camouflage to avoid detection. Flight typical of grouse family, but fast and will fly up and down steep slopes quickly and easily. Food is almost entirely plant matter, mainly shoots, leaves and berries of heathland plants, also buds, twigs and seeds of trees like birch where available. Diet varies with seasonal availability of foods; will dig through snow in winter to get to food plants.
Nests invariably on ground; generally in open, partly sheltered by rock or taller vegetation.

Similar species

Characteristic white wings and underbody, together with habitat preferences, easily distinguish Ptarmigan from other British grouse species.

Shooting season

J F M A M J J A S O N D

88

CAPERCAILLIE

Tetrao urogallus
size: ♂ 84–90 cm (33–35 in)
      ♀ 58–64 cm (23–25 in)

LEK DISPLAY POSTURE

Field identification

Very large grouse, with broad wings and rounded tail. ♂ 30 per cent larger than ♀; has overall dark plumage, body and head basically slate-grey and black with glossy blue-green breast; wings dark, rich brown; under-parts and tail marked with white. ♀ mottled with black, light grey and buff; dark brown upper-parts; characteristic rufous patch on breast contrasts with lighter under-parts. Juvenile generally similar to adult ♀.
Voice: ♂ silent outside breeding season; ♀ call note a loud, harsh *kcock*.

Inhabits chiefly mature coniferous woodland in upland areas; prefers mixture of fairly dense tree cover with thick undergrowth and open ground, especially moorland. Resident, but some local movements in winter, particularly by ♂♂.

Habitat and distribution

Usually ground-dwelling in summer and autumn; found in trees during winter. Breaks cover noisily, but flight quick, silent and usually brief; rarely flies above tree-top height. Typical gamebird flight, series of quick wing-beats alternating with glides on decurved wings, with neck extended. Food almost entirely vegetable material, varying with seasonal availability from shoots and buds of conifers from late autumn to early spring; including a range of grasses, clover, berries, seeds, etc during the rest of year.
Nests on ground in dense cover in forest, juniper scrub, occasionally in deep heather on open moor.

Behaviour and feeding

Adult ♂ unmistakable with characteristic dark plumage and large size. ♀ may be confused with ♀ Red or Black Grouse, but is much larger than both.

Similar species

J	F	M	A	M	J	J	A	S	O	N	D
	31							1			

Shooting season

89

WOODPIGEON

Columba palumbus
size: 41 cm (16 in)

Field identification

Large, heavy pigeon, characterised by broad white band across wing seen readily in flight, and white patches on sides of neck. Sexes similar. Body plumage basically blue-grey, head and neck bluer than rest, flanks and underside paler; purple-green gloss to sides of neck. Young duller and lack white on wings and neck.
Voice: characteristic rhythmic, muffled *cooing* calls.

Chiefly occurs in cultivated areas and woodlands, but also in towns and cities. Feeds on farmland and uses trees and hedges to roost and nest. British breeding population mainly resident, with some local movements and emigration to north-west Europe; passage migrants and winter visitors from continent appear during October/November to **Habitat and distribution** March/April, mainly in eastern England.

Behaviour and feeding

Normally feeds during daylight on ground in open cultivated land or woodland glades; makes extensive use of agricultural crops particularly in autumn and winter, including spilt grain on stubble, turnips, brassicas, clover, etc; also takes buds, young leaves and flowers in spring. Gregarious outside breeding season; commonly feeds in very large flocks; roosts communally in woodland or hedgerows. When flushed rises with loud clatter of wings; strong flight usually direct and rapid. Nest site varies, but normally in woodland or hedgerow trees; occasionally building, rock ledges, rarely on ground.

Similar species

Confusion most likely with Stock Dove, Rock Dove and some domestic pigeons (all protected), but all are smaller and lack white wing and neck patches of Woodpigeon.

Shooting season

J F M A M J J A S O N D

CROW
Corvus corone
size: 47 cm (18½ in)

CARRION CROW   HOODED CROW

Two races of this large corvid occur in the British Isles. The Carrion Crow (*C.c.corone*) has uniform sleek black plumage with a greenish or blue-purple gloss. The Hooded Crow (*C.c.cornix*) is black except for grey back and under-parts. Both have a heavy, dark brown bill, and square tail.
Voice: characteristic harsh, croaking *caw*.

Field identification

Hooded Crow

Carrion Crow

Habitat and distribution

Carrion Crow resident; population augmented by some winter immigrants from western Europe. Breeding range overlaps with Hooded Crow in north and east Scotland, where hybrids frequently occur. Hooded Crow resident in Scotland. Winter visitors from Baltic and Scandinavia occur mainly in eastern and central England during October/November to March/April. Found in a wide range of habitats from open moors and heaths, pasture and arable farmland, to parkland, wooded country, and coastlands.

Relatively solitary, and most frequently found singly or in pairs; very occasionally in small flocks, particularly at roosts. Flight usually direct, with slow deliberate wing-beats; rarely soars. Feeds chiefly on the ground in open country, walking or occasionally hopping while it forages. Crows are opportunist feeders and diet consequently differs with area and time of year; extremely varied food includes vegetable matter, carrion, small mammals, birds and eggs, amphibians, insects, etc.
Trees preferred for nesting, but will use low bushes, cliff ledges or on ground (usually on islets).

Behaviour and feeding

Hooded Crow unmistakable, although flight silhouette like Carrion Crow. Carrion Crow may be confused with Rook; other black corvids are the much larger Raven (protected), and smaller Chough (protected), both of which have very distinctive calls.

Similar species

J F M A M J J A S O N D

Shooting season

ROOK

Corvus frugilegus
size: 46 cm (18 in)

Field identification

Large, black corvid with characteristic bare, white face-patch. Loose plumage around flanks gives 'shaggy trousers' appearance. Feathers have iridescent blue-purple or greenish gloss; slender, pointed bill is grey-black. Juvenile birds lack bare face patch, but characterised by loose flank feathers.
Voice: wide range of calls, but typically a fairly soft *kaw*.

Chiefly in agricultural areas with suitable nesting trees. Forages in both pasture and cultivated land. Commonly close to small settlements, mainly in lowlands, and absent from urban areas. British birds resident; population supplemented by influx of winter immigrants from Scandinavia and central Europe, particularly to eastern Britain during October/November, departing late February/April.

Habitat and distribution

Behaviour and feeding

Highly gregarious throughout the year. Normally encountered in small parties or flocks up to several hundred birds; in autumn and winter often roosts in very large numbers, frequently with Jackdaws.
Flight direct with regular, rapid wing-beats; sometimes glides and soars; flocks fly in loose formation. Walks easily, hopping occasionally. Feeds in open on the ground. Diet chiefly comprises vegetable matter, especially cereals, root crops, fruits, etc; animal food mostly gathered from grassland, primarily earthworms and leatherjackets obtained by probing the top layer of soil. Will also take a variety of invertebrates, carrion, small mammals, young birds and eggs.
Nests colonially, at traditional sites; normally in large trees, but not within extensive woodland areas; exceptionally on man-made structures. Most frequently uses beech, oak, elm, Scots pine and sycamore trees.

Similar species

May be confused with Carrion Crow. Some resemblance to Raven (protected) and Chough (protected), but these have distinctive call notes.

J	F	M	A	M	J	J	A	S	O	N	D

Shooting season

92

JACKDAW

Corvus monedula
size: 33 cm (13 in)

Small, dark corvid, characterised by grey nape and ear-coverts; under-parts dark grey, remaining plumage black. Distinctive pale grey eye, and short bill.
Voice: characteristic short, high-pitched, metallic *tchak*.

Field identification

Frequents a wide variety of relatively open habitats, from parkland and farmland to sea-cliffs, towers and old buildings, etc. Forages mainly in pasture land. British population generally sedentary, although some local movements and emigration to continent recorded. Winter immigrants from Europe appear during October/November to late February/April.

Habitat and distribution

Highly sociable corvid, often in large flocks and frequently associates with Rooks and Starlings when foraging in pastures. Moves on ground with quick, jerky walk; appears more alert and 'perky' than other corvids. Highly adaptable, omnivorous feeder; diet varies considerably with location and time of year. Spends much time feeding on surface insects in grassland; grain and wild plant seeds form an important part of vegetable matter eaten. Also takes legumes, earthworms, birds' eggs and nestlings, and carrion.
Usually nests in a hole in tree, building, rock face, etc; also constructs nest in trees.

Behaviour and feeding

Most likely confusion is with Chough (protected), but this species has distinctive flight and call-notes. Carrion and Hooded Crows, Raven (protected) and Rook all much larger and heavier than Jackdaw.

Similar species

J F M A M J J A S O N D

Shooting season

MAGPIE

Pica pica
size: 46 cm (18 in)

Field identification

Medium-sized corvid, characterised by distinctive black and white plumage and long wedge-shaped tail (comprising 50 per cent of total length). Belly, flanks and scapulars white; rest of plumage black with blueish or greenish gloss. Sexes alike; juvenile a duller version of adult. *Voice*: an unmistakable harsh, loud, repetitive *chak-chak-chak*, easily heard at long range.

Habitat and distribution

Resident; chiefly in farmland and open country with hedges and trees, also urban parks, suburban gardens, etc.

Behaviour and feeding

Found singly, in pairs or small parties; some flocking occurs; in autumn and winter roosts. Flight direct, with rapid wing-beats. Feeds primarily on ground, walking or hopping, and usually close to cover, in woodland rides, adjacent to hedgerows, etc. Diet varied, including insects, carrion and vegetable matter, especially grain, berries, fruits, etc; predates nests containing eggs and young of small birds; takes small birds and mammals, and a variety of molluscs, earthworms, etc.
Prefers nesting in tall trees and bushes, commonly ash, oak, hawthorn, sycamore and alder; will use cliffs and crags if no suitable trees available; nest of sticks and earth frequently domed with thorny branches.

Similar species

Both adults and juveniles unmistakable, with distinctive plumage and voice.

Shooting season

J	F	M	A	M	J	J	A	S	O	N	D

JAY

Garrulus glandarius
size: 34 cm (13½ in)

Medium-sized corvid, characterised by white rump, black tail and white wing-patch conspicuous in flight. Body pinkish-brown; bright blue and black barred wing coverts; black and white erectile crown feathers; fairly long tail and short, rounded wings.
Voice: characteristic harsh, screeching call, very loud and detectable over long distances.

Field identification

Primarily an inhabitant of oak woodlands, but found in variety of fairly open deciduous woodlands and coverts with good secondary growth, also mixed and coniferous woods, suburban gardens and parks, orchards, etc. British birds mainly resident, but local movements do occur; winter immigrants from Baltic and North Sea countries of continental Europe – often resulting from invasion movements rather than regular migratory movements – recorded mostly in south-east England.

Habitat and distribution

Rarely outside woods; moves in tree-canopy by jumping among branches; usually hops on the ground. Flies easily among trees, but in open flight appears weak and laboured with jerky, flapping action. Commonly in small parties or flocks outside breeding season.
Acorns predominate in autumn diet, and large numbers stored for winter feeding, hence close association with oak woodlands; other vegetable matter includes fruits, also grain and legumes; animal food includes young birds and (especially) eggs, and woodland insects.
Nests in trees, in more secluded parts of broadleaved or coniferous woodland.

Behaviour and feeding

Easily identified by voice and plumage characteristics plus habitat preference.

Similar species

J   F   M   A   M   J   J   A   S   O   N   D

Shooting season

BROWN HARE

MOUNTAIN HARE
(winter coat)

RABBIT

GREY SQUIRREL

BROWN (or FIELD) HARE

Lepus capensis
size: 50–68 cm (20–27 in)

Medium-sized mammal characterised by very long ears and long hind-legs. Ears have black tips; body colour yellowish- to reddish-brown in summer, becoming greyer in winter; upper tail is black.

Field identification

Primarily a lowland species; prefers open, relatively flat country, especially farmland, and also deciduous woodland. Extends to higher moors in some areas, where range overlaps with Mountain Hare. Introduced into Ireland.

Habitat and distribution

Mainly nocturnal and solitary. Moves very fast over the ground, leaping with legs fully stretched; frequently zig-zags, especially when bolting if disturbed from form. Feeds on a wide range of vegetation, including agricultural crops – and young forestry plantings.
Form may be in tall grass, scrub, woodland or open fields, and is normally well sheltered.

Behaviour and feeding

26TH. Sept.

28 Feb.

Resembles Mountain Hare and similar to, but much larger than, Rabbit.

Similar species

J	F	M	A	M	J	J	A	S	O	N	D

Shooting season

MOUNTAIN (or BLUE) HARE

Lepus timidus
size: 45–55 cm (18–22 in)

Medium-sized mammal characterised by long, black-tipped ears, and long hind-legs; tail lacks any black colouring. Body colour grey-brown to reddish-brown in summer; in winter largely white with black ear-tips, although not all individuals change colour, and in Ireland none attain white coat; during moult mixtures of white and grey-brown (or blueish-brown) occur.

Field identification

Mainly found in upland areas of Britain, but also on lower ground in Ireland (where it largely replaces the Brown Hare). Inhabits both open hillsides and mountain habitats, and woodlands, including forestry plantations.

Habitat and distribution

97

Behaviour and feeding	Normally fairly solitary, but may be found in small groups. Often active during daylight. Moves with leaping gait; when running tends to take a fairly direct line with little zig-zagging. Feeds on a wide variety of vegetation, including the bark and tops of young trees – occasionally inflicting serious damage to plantations. Form normally amongst boulders or rocks, or grass tussocks.
Similar species	Mountain Hare (except in winter coat) closely resembles Brown Hare, and is similar to the much smaller Rabbit.

J   F   M   A   M   J   J   A   S   O   N   D

Shooting season

Oryctolagus cuniculus
size: 34–45 cm (13–18 in)

RABBIT

Field identification

Medium-sized mammal characterised by long ears and long hind-legs; short, woolly tail which is white on underside contrasting with black or brown-grey above. Body colour normally light brown, but wide range of colour varieties occur, notably black, fawn, white and silver-grey. (Shown in colour on p. 96.)

Found chiefly on light, sandy soils in open habitats – heaths, sand dunes, moorland, etc; also in woodland; generally not at higher elevations.
Local variations in population densities are largely controlled by outbreaks of the disease myxomatosis.

Habitat and distribution

Behaviour and feeding Most active in evening, also feed during afternoon and at night. Moves with bounding gait; runs quickly, turning at sharp angles. Burrows extensively (only the doe actually excavates); lives colonially in warrens; occasionally lives above ground (especially young bucks). Feeds mainly on grass and other green herbage; frequently causes damage to farm and garden crops when local populations high in numbers; will gnaw tree bark, especially in winter and with a preference for saplings.
Capable of breeding throughout year, but mainly spring and early summer; young born in burrow dug away from main colony.

Similar species Both Brown and Mountain Hares are larger, with longer ears and larger hind-legs.

J   F   M   A   M   J   J   A   S   O   N   D

Shooting season

GREY SQUIRREL

Sciurus carolinensis
size: 45–55 cm (17½–21½ in)

Medium sized rodent. Characterised by long, bushy tail (nearly half total length); grey fur with some reddish and yellow tinges on back and flanks; and absence of prominent ear tufts. Under-parts white; gains silver-grey winter coat usually in late autumn, and shorter, brownish summer coat in spring. (Shown in colour on p. 96.)

Field identification

Introduced into Britain during late 19th and early 20th centuries; widespread by 1950s. Chiefly in deciduous woodland, particularly with oak, beech, chestnut and hazel. Also parkland, suburban gardens, etc; mainly in lowland areas; less frequently in coniferous woodland.

Habitat and distribution

Active during the day, particularly in early morning. Moves quickly on the ground with bounding gait. Varied diet includes grain, herbage and animal material. Plant components of diet dominated by nuts and other tree seed (including beech-mast), also leaves, buds, shoots, etc; strips bark to eat woody tissue (inflicting considerable damage in the process); animal material includes small birds, nestlings and eggs; also takes insects and fungi.

Behaviour and feeding

Resembles Red Squirrel (protected), although the latter is smaller, more lightly-built and mainly in coniferous woodland.

Similar species

J	F	M	A	M	J	J	A	S	O	N	D

Shooting season

FLOCK PATTERNS

MALLARD

TEAL

WIGEON

PINTAIL

SHOVELER

GADWALL

TUFTED DUCK

POCHARD

GOLDENEYE

Roughshooting

The term 'roughshooting' embraces all forms of sporting shotgun shooting other than formal driven game shooting (see Chapter 8) and coastal duck, goose and wader shooting (see Chapter 9). It therefore includes the pursuit of game, pigeons, Rabbit, hares, Snipe and inland duck and geese.

The pursuit of these quarry species can provide some of the most demanding and exciting sport to be found in this country; as with any form of sporting shooting, to be successful you must understand the habits of your quarry and these are explained briefly in the chapter on Quarry Identification.

Good roughshooting can be enjoyed on a small acreage of land, dependent upon the type and distribution of habitat. The form in which roughshooting takes place will largely be determined by the nature of the ground and by the quarry species being pursued.

WILDFOWL INLAND

Most rough shoots either provide or have the potential to provide an opportunity for inland duck shooting. If suitable ponds or wetlands do not exist then these can be created. The best opportunities for inland duck shooting come from either flighting a pond at dusk or by intercepting birds as they flight between their roosting and feeding areas. Good duck shooting can also be enjoyed when duck, particularly Mallard, flight onto stubble fields during September and early October. This can be done at night, particularly for a few nights either side of the full moon when there is sufficient moonlight and a light cloud covering against which the birds will be clearly silhouetted. If any area of the roughshooter's land floods after prolonged rainfall, he should keep an eye open for preened feathers and droppings; if these signs of duck occur, he should be prepared to take advantage of the fortuitous opportunity for flighting in that area.

The roughshooter's opportunity to pursue geese inland will be largely restricted to the occasional skein of Whitefronts and to the increasingly more numerous Canada Geese which roost on reservoirs and lakes, where they can be particularly tame; but to lie in wait for them on their flight lines can be most exciting. The younger birds make excellent eating.

Snipe can provide some of the most testing shooting for the roughshooter and may be walked up or, most difficult of all, flighted at dusk as they come to a marshy spot to feed.

RABBIT SHOOTING

At one time Rabbits were the mainstay of the roughshooter's bag, but the introduction of myxomatosis in the early 50s largely decimated the Rabbit population. Whilst myxomatosis still occurs in certain areas, throughout a large part of the country the Rabbit is once again on the increase.

Rabbits may be shot for sport in a number of ways. It is hardly necessary to describe the hunting out of hedgerows, patches of bracken and other cover with a dog. The method to be adopted will depend on the ability of the shooter to work his dog to the best advantage over a particular piece of ground. How Rabbits can best be dealt with must be decided by those on the spot. Only the man with local knowledge gained from experience will know the place where Rabbits will be most likely to be found, from which side of the hedgerow they are more likely to bolt into the open; and from what haven of safety, whether it be burrows or thick cover, they are likely to be flushed. Although most popularly known as a burrowing creature, Rabbits will lie out for weeks in fields which provide some sort of cover such as thistles or roots. If Rabbits are not walked up with a dog they can be stalked or ambushed as they emerge from their burrows to feed at evening time.

Ferreting is a particularly effective means of controlling the numbers of Rabbits, but to go into details of ferreting is outside the scope of this book other than to say that no Rabbit should ever be shot at the mouth of the hole as the ferret bringing up the rear will be endangered. Rabbits should always be allowed to get a short distance from the burrow as a wounded one may well crawl down the hole—even a 'dead' Rabbit can kick itself a couple of yards.

WOODPIGEON SHOOTING

The Woodpigeon offers the roughshooter good sport, a cheap and tasty meal and a battle of wits throughout the year. The two main methods of shooting are roost shooting and decoying. The method chosen will depend on the time of year, the availability of food supplies and the type of countryside over which the rough-shooter is operating. Roost shooting is primarily a winter activity and involves the shooter getting underneath the flightline of birds approaching the woodland or copse where they are going to roost at night or rest in the daytime.

For the majority of pigeon shooters, decoying as opposed to roost shooting is the main sport. Decoying can be enjoyed all the year round and depends only on the food supplies available. A good knowledge of the pigeons preferred diet and reconnaissance are two essential prerequisites for successful pigeon shooting. The B.A.S.C. publication *Know Your Woodpigeon Shooting* is recommended reading on this topic.

GAME

Roughshooting for game is normally an activity undertaken by one or two shooters with a dog working hedgerows or ditches or may involve a larger party of guns walking-up. It is particularly important to always ensure that a shoot leader is appointed and that every member of the line retains his place in relation to the people on either side of him and that the line is kept straight.

A CODE OF CONDUCT FOR ROUGHSHOOTING

WHERE

Always ensure that you are authorised to shoot where you intend to go and that you know precisely where the shoot boundaries are located.

You should be aware of any public rights of way crossing the land over which you are shooting.

Always advise the owner and/or tenant in good time if you want to go shooting and check that it is convenient.

WHAT

Always confirm with the owner and tenant what quarry you may shoot.

An invitation to shoot over a piece of land will not always necessarily entail an invitation to shoot any quarry species.

It is important that you know precisely what species you may pursue.

Always ensure you have a valid game licence if shooting at game; carry it and your shotgun certificate with you.

EQUIPMENT

Always use suitably loaded cartridges for your quarry.

The combination of gun, cartridge, and choke is important, and will be influenced by personal preference.

The table is for standard 12-bore loads; smaller bore guns will have shorter effective ranges.

Shot size	Quarry	Maximum effective range
No 4/5	Ducks	35m (about 40yd)
No 5/6	Hares & Rabbit	35m (about 40yd)
No 6/7	Pigeon/Woodcock/Partridge/Teal/Grouse/Pheasant	35m (about 40yd)
No 8	Snipe	35m (about 40yd)

IN THE FIELD

Always ensure your companions know your position and observe safe shooting angles.

If shooting in company, appoint a leader and always ensure that each member of the party knows the plan for the day.

Always identify your quarry and ensure that it is safe to shoot.

Make sure that you know what is beyond the target.

Always condemn unsporting shooting, that is at poor fliers and at birds out of range.

When engaged in vermin shooting or crop protection, shooting at poor fliers may be acceptable. Out-of-range shooting, whether at game or vermin species, is *not* acceptable.

Always seek to present your quarry as a sporting shot, giving it reasonable 'law'; this means that the flushing dog or ferret is not endangered.

'Law' in this context means to allow the quarry to gain sufficient distance from you to present both a safe and sporting shot.

Always respect the owner's property, crops, livestock and fences and follow the country code.

Open gates rather than climb them, and close them after you. Climb a secured gate at the hinged end. Never break rails, fences or hedges. Never walk in standing corn. Avoid disturbance to livestock; keep your dog under control.

Always be especially vigilant about keeping in a straight line when walking in thick cover or dead ground.

The going may be easy for you, but slow and difficult for your companions.

Never shoot at a bird just because it is in the range of your gun. It may present a more sporting shot for one of your companions.

Never shoot at partially obscured quarry.

Never be greedy. Do not shoot more than you can carry or really need. Do not overshoot; a viable breeding stock must be left on the ground at the end of the season.

Crop protection may be an exception.

If a bird is shot and falls over the boundary, it is proper to seek permission to retrieve it.

Good relationships with sporting 'neighbours' are very important.

Never take your gun with you unless you have been authorised.

Never leave litter, take your empty cartridge cases home.

If you have been shooting from a hide, make sure that the area is left in such a way that no one can tell that you have been there.

AT THE END OF THE DAY
Always ensure that you have collected up all your equipment.

Always leave the place tidy.

It is courteous to thank the owner or occupier and to offer him something from the bag.

Always attend to your dog before yourself.

If the journey home is a long one, your dog may appreciate a drink before you leave.

Always inspect your dog for thorns and cuts.

Treat them promptly.

Always take your quarry from the game bag as soon as possible. Store it in a cool fly-proof place. Do not waste it.

Always clean your gun before putting it away; check it over for faults which may need attention.

Have any faults attended to immediately.

Walking up

Formal driven game shooting is a highly organised aspect of the sport of shooting in which 'Game' birds are driven by beaters over or towards a line of standing guns.

Gamebirds, as defined by the Game Act 1831, are Pheasants, Partridges, Grouse, Heath and Moor Game (Ptarmigan) and Black Game (Black Grouse).

Historically, game was shot by 'walking up' and shooting birds as they flew away, but in the mid-to-late 1800s, coinciding with the general introduction of breech loaders, a change occurred and the guns stood whilst the birds were driven over them by beaters. This became a very institutionalised and formal aspect of the sport around which a strict code of conduct, or etiquette, has now evolved.

Ptarmigan are normally only shot when walking up, and are therefore outside the scope of this chapter.

WHERE

There is no free game shooting in the United Kingdom and shooting rights over any piece of land are always legally held by someone.

There are many ways of organising the management of game shooting rights. The most common are:

1. The landowner may retain the game shooting rights for himself and organise the shooting for the benefit of himself and his guests.

2. The landowner may retain the shooting rights for himself, but invite a limited number of outside guns to each pay a set sum of money to have a gun in the shoot for one season. This system helps the shoot owner to defray the costs of running the shoot.

3. The landowner may retain the shooting rights himself and each season sell a number of shooting days to outside guns who each pay for one day's shooting. This is another way of defraying costs.

4. The landowner may lease the game-shooting rights to an individual who then becomes responsible for the financing and running of the shooting in any way he wishes.

5. The landowner may lease the shooting rights to a 'syndicate' of guns who take on the full responsibility of financing and organising the shooting in any way they wish.

6. An individual or a group of people or 'Company' (i.e. a sporting agency) may buy the shooting rights over one or more parcels of land in perpetuity or for a set period of time, and run the shooting in any way they wish.

7. A sporting agency may lease the shooting rights and 'sell' shooting days to outside guns.

Most formal shoots vary from about 400 up to several thousand acres in size.

As will be seen from the above, there is no set pattern as to how the management of shooting rights is organised, it being up to the owner or the lessee of the shooting rights to decide what system suits him best.

WHEN

The open and close seasons for game shooting are defined by the Game Act 1831. The open seasons are:

SHOOTING SEASONS

England, Wales and Scotland

Pheasant	1 October–1 February inclusive
Partridge	1 September–1 February inclusive
Grouse/Ptarmigan	12 August–10 December inclusive
Blackgame	20 August–10 December inclusive
Snipe*	12 August–31 January inclusive
Woodcock*	1 October–31 January inclusive (England and Wales)
	1 September–31 January inclusive (Scotland)

*Requires a Game Licence, but is not 'Game' within the meaning of the Game Act 1831.

NORTHERN IRELAND

The shooting seasons and quarry species differ from those in England, Wales and Scotland. They are subject to yearly change (for example, Partridge and hen Pheasants are currently protected).

At the peg

CODE OF PRACTICE

THE SHOOT ORGANISER'S OBLIGATIONS

Always remember your responsibility to safeguard your quarry and its environment for future generations.

Always remember that others will judge the sport by your behaviour and that of your companions.

Always ensure you have made adequate provision for finding lost game, either by inviting your guests to use their own gundogs, or by arranging for an appropriate number of 'pickers-up'.

Always ensure that if transport is needed between drives for guns and beaters, that it is adequate for the purpose and safe.

The quality of the sport is more important than pure numbers, and one should endeavour to produce truly sporting shots.

Always make provision for the proper treatment of shot game by ensuring that it is hung up in the 'game cart' to cool quickly, kept clean, dry and stored in a cool flyproof larder.

It is good management to see that both guns and beaters have somewhere dry to eat their lunch and that water is available for gundogs.

The arrangements for the day and the marking out of the stands should be agreed with the keeper well beforehand.

The organisation of the day is your responsibility: make sure everybody knows what is expected of them.

THE GUEST'S OBLIGATIONS

Always reply promptly to an invitation to shoot.

Make sure you know whether you are expected to take your dog and your lunch; also ensure that you know the time and place to meet.

Always remember that it is the sportsman's responsibility to understand the laws relating to his sport; in particular to be able to recognise his quarry and know when and where he may shoot.

Always arrive punctually.

Always wear a hat, sensible footwear and suitable clothing to suit your surroundings.

Always keep your gun in its cover between drives and while travelling in vehicles.

Always go to your stand quickly and quietly and check where the other guns are placed.

Acknowledge the gun on either side of you, or any 'stops' or pickers-up by raising your hat or hand, but not by calling out.

A 'stop' is someone who is positioned in order to stop game running or breaking out to the side of the drive.

Always check the direction the beaters will come from, the position of stops and where the pickers-up are placed.

Always check if there is any agricultural work in progress in your vicinity.

Always remain quiet at your peg, and do not move from where you were placed, unless so instructed by your host.

Always condemn unsporting shooting, i.e. at poor flyers and birds out of range.

Always 'mark' all game shot and collect those near your peg at the end of the drive.

Either use your own dog, or tell a picker-up the numbers and whereabouts of lost or wounded game so that they can be quickly brought to hand and despatched. A sharp knock on the head with a suitably heavy stick or priest is recommended.

Always ask your host what game is to be shot, and the position regarding ground game and vermin.

Always ask how many guns are shooting and, if you draw for a number, how the system works.

At most shoots, pegs will be numbered 1–8; No 1 is usually on the right and No 8 on the left of the drive. The normal practice is to move up two numbers for each consecutive drive. Make sure you know what number peg you should be at for each drive.

Always ensure you have a valid game licence, and carry it and your shotgun certificate with you.

A responsible shot will have Third Party Liability Insurance cover. B.A.S.C. membership provides this.

Never bring a guest with you without first confirming that you may.

Never be afraid to seek advice on any aspect relating to the conduct of the day.

Never take long shots, or shoot at partially obscured game.

Never load your gun until the drive commences and unload as soon as it is finished.

Never shoot between drives.

Never shoot low in front when the beaters are approaching.

Never let excitement cloud your judgement.

Never shoot behind without first taking the gun from your shoulder, keeping the barrels pointing vertically.

Never be greedy. Just because a bird is in range of your gun does not necessarily make it yours; it may produce a more sporting shot for one of your companions.

GUNS AND CARTRIDGES

Always use suitably loaded cartridges for your quarry.

If shooting with a pair of guns, make sure you and your loader have practised the method of changing guns. The person passing the gun will hold it in his right hand at the grip with the barrels pointing upwards; the person receiving the gun will take it in his left hand by the fore-end. The safety catch should be on 'safe' throughout.

The combination of gun, cartridge and choke is important, and will be influenced by personal preference.

Shot Size	Quarry	Maximum Effective Range
No 6/7	Grouse Partridge Pheasant Woodcock	35m (about 40yd)

Remember that relatively little choke is needed for game shooting. The recommendations are for standard 12-bore loads; smaller bore guns will have shorter effective ranges.

Always thank the keepers, beaters and pickers-up as it is largely their efforts which have provided your sport.

It is customary always to tip the head keeper, but if in doubt check with your host.

Always take care of any game which you have been given. Do not waste it.

Always ensure that you have collected up all your equipment.

Always thank your host for your days sport, and as an extra courtesy write and thank him later.

Always feed and water your dog before yourself and check him over for thorns and cuts.

Clean your gun, and check it for faults which may need rectifying.

Have any faults attended to immediately by a competent gunsmith.

For many centuries duck, goose and wader shooting has been part of life on estuaries around our coast. The participant was and still is referred to as a wildfowler and he continues to follow old traditions established by professional wildfowlers. Wildfowling is purely a sport now, with sportsmen in pursuit of a restricted number of the edible quarry species. Normally the sportsman is on foot, but in some circumstances boats are used. It is a thoroughly modern recreation; it rewards the correct use of ancient skills as well as the understanding of nature. It requires toughness and perseverance. It can provide comradeship and a source of food.

Purists will argue that true wildfowling is strictly a coastal activity, taking place below the high-water mark – that is, on the foreshore around the coast. However, duck and goose flighting does take place inland on marshes, lakes and specifically managed flight-ponds and many mallard are reared, released and shot on shoots throughout the country.

WILDFOWLING TODAY

There is very little free wildfowling in Britain today, since shooting rights are almost always held by landowners or shooting tenants under a measure of control defined principally by the Game Act 1831, Game (Scotland) Act 1832 and the Firearms Act 1968.

England, Wales and Northern Ireland: definition of foreshore

In England, Wales and Northern Ireland the traditional place for wildfowling is that part of the seashore which is more often than not covered by the flux and reflux of the four ordinary tides occurring midway between spring and neap tides. This is called the foreshore and much of it is in Crown ownership or subject to control by the holders of regulating leases from the Crown Estate Commissioners. The remaining areas are in private hands. In England, Wales and Northern Ireland the British Association for Shooting and Conservation has an agreement with the Crown Estate Commissioners (and with the Duchy of Lancaster) whereby its members have been granted authority to be on foreshore controlled by the Crown or Duchy of Lancaster with a shotgun and therefore they have a sound defence should a prosecution be brought against them for armed trespass. Elsewhere, it must be stressed, permission is required to shoot on private foreshore; and the onus is on the wildfowler to establish whether the foreshore is private. Access and egress must be by public right of way unless otherwise authorised, preferably in writing. The only rights for members of the public on foreshores in England, Wales and Northern Ireland are those of fishing and navigation.

Scotland: definition of foreshore

In Scotland the foreshore is defined slightly differently as the area between high- and low-water marks of ordinary spring tides. In Scotland, whether the ownership pertains to the Crown or a private individual, the Crown retains in trust for the public certain rights, including recreation, on the foreshore (except on Orkney and the Shetlands) by virtue of which members of the public may engage in wildfowling. This public right may only be taken away by statute as, for example, by the establishment of nature reserves under the National Parks and Access to the Countryside Acts 1949, by declaration of areas of special protection under the Wildlife and Countryside Act 1981, or the establishment of country parks under the Countryside (Scotland) Act 1967 and Countryside Act 1968. As before, the onus is on the wildfowler to establish whether such statutory controls exist.

UNDERSTANDING THE HABITS OF YOUR QUARRY

Ducks

Generally ducks feed by night, flighting between feeding and resting places at dawn and dusk. On the foreshore ducks will also feed in daylight and their habits will be affected by the tide. The stronger the tide, the rougher the water and the more marked will be the movement of birds.

Geese

Geese feed by day, flighting between the feeding and resting places at dawn and dusk. On moonlit nights, however, some species, in particular Pinkfooted and White-fronted geese, will flight back to their feeding grounds from their roost. The roost may be a large expanse of inland water or on the open shore or sea. During the few nights around full moon they may even remain on the feeding grounds throughout the whole period.

Waders

Movement of wading birds is largely based on the tides, feeding as they do almost exclusively on the intertidal zone. Golden Plover is the only quarry wader species (other than Snipe and Woodcock) and they regularly flight inland and feed on pastures.

Coastal Shooting

Coastal shooting provides immense variety; when high winds and rough weather prevail, tide flighting or decoying Wigeon on the flashes, which often remain after the tide has ebbed, can provide some of the season's most exciting sport. Wigeon flight well under the moon, too.

Successful wildfowlers rarely achieve satisfactory bags without acquiring a detailed knowledge of local conditions. This includes information about the prevailing and expected weather, the tides and their combined effect on the flighting and feeding habits of the birds. Such observations can be every bit as fascinating as the actual shooting. Binoculars are an essential piece of equipment.

At the beginning of the season, which starts on 1 September, the foreshore shooter will expect to see wildfowl and waders which have bred in Britain. At dawn and dusk Mallard and Teal will establish flight lines to and from their inland feeding grounds.

At this time, since many Mallard will be feeding on corn stubbles, the wildfowler will endeavour to place himself strategically where he can intercept their flight. During these early weeks of the season the birds, such as barley-fed Mallard, are at their best for eating.

By October the migratory duck and geese will have started to arrive in large numbers. Most estuaries are visited by small parties of migratory Mallard, Wigeon, Teal and Pintail to supplement the resident populations of Mallard and Teal.

Once wintry weather prevails, the wildfowler is in his element; the best results are often achieved when conditions are at their worst. Strong winds in particular keep the wildfowl on the move in an effort to find shelter, and when the fresh inland marshes freeze up, wildfowl are forced to move to more open coastal areas.

Under prolonged and extreme wintry weather, hungry birds rapidly lose body condition and become more approachable – thus no longer a worthy quarry. At such times the true sportsman has no need to be told when to use restraint, but the Wildlife and Countryside Act 1981 empowers the Secretary of State to invoke a statutory ban on wildfowling until the conditions have improved and the birds fully recovered.

Setting out decoys

Always know where you can shoot by understanding the definition of foreshore in the area where you intend to shoot.

You must understand the definition of foreshore as given on page 113.

Always know what you can shoot and be capable of identifying common quarry that you intend to shoot.

Those who shoot on the foreshore can only legally take the birds listed in Schedule 2 Part I of the *Wildlife and Countryside Act 1981* unless otherwise authorised. Schedule 2 Part I lists those wild birds which may legally be shot during the open season. (See Appendix 4 on page 139.)

Schedule 2 Part II refers to those birds which may be killed or taken at any time by authorised persons; you should be aware that some bye-laws, for example on nature reserves, do not include the shooting of birds in Schedule 2 Part II.

WILDFOWL SEASONS

Always know when you can shoot the quarry you intend to pursue.

England, Scotland and Wales
Inland: 1 September – 31 January inc.
Below the mean high-water mark of ordinary spring tides: 1 September – 20 February inc.
NB Geese and Ducks only, *not* Waders, after 31 January.

Northern Ireland
The shooting seasons and quarry species differ from those in England, Scotland and Wales and are subject to yearly change; for example, Canada Geese are currently protected. There is no shooting on the foreshore after 31 January and night shooting is prohibited.

The shooting of wildfowl on Sunday is illegal in some areas.

Counties and County Boroughs in England and Wales in which there is no Sunday shooting of Schedule 2 Part I. Birds: Anglesey, Brecknock, Caernarvon, Cardigan, Carmarthen, Cornwall, Denbigh, Devon, Doncaster, Glamorgan, Great

Yarmouth, Isle of Ely, Leeds, Merioneth, Norfolk, Pembroke, Somerset, Yorkshire (North Riding), Yorkshire (West Riding).

NB The Counties referred to are those which were in existence before local government re-organisation in the early 1970's. It is the sportsman's responsibility to check whether or not Sunday shooting is allowed in the area he wishes to wildfowl.

There is no shooting of wildfowl in Scotland on Sundays or Christmas Day.

Never shoot from a mechanically propelled boat.

It is illegal to shoot from a mechanically propelled boat in the immediate pursuit of wildfowl. The prudent wildfowler will, therefore, dispense with the engine altogether.

COASTAL SHOOTING

Guns and Cartridges

Always choose a gun that is suitable for the type of shooting you intend to pursue.

A double-barrelled 12-bore is a suitable all round shotgun. If your fieldcraft is good, you will be successful with the standard 67.5 mm (2½ in) cartridge (correctly loaded). Traditionally, wildfowlers prefer a 75 mm (3 in) chambered gun which enables them to shoot heavier shot more effectively. Big bore guns, i.e. 10, 8 and 4 bores, although capable of handling big shot very effectively can be cumbersome and a burden. Choke only marginally increases effective range and is no excuse for attempting out-of-range shots.

The use of any gun or rifle firing a single bullet for the purpose of killing wildfowl, whilst not prohibited by law, is not an accepted sporting practice, and is discouraged by the B.A.S.C. for its members. The Wildlife and Countryside Act 1981 prohibits the use of automatic and semi-automatic shotguns for wildfowling unless they are restricted to fire not more than three cartridges in succession without reloading.

Always choose a cartridge suitable for the type of shooting you intend to pursue.

The following shot sizes are recommended:

Shot Size	Quarry	Maximum effective range
No 4/5	Ducks	35 m (about 40 yd)
No 6	Teal/	
	Waders	35 m (about 40 yd)
BB No 1		
or No 3	Geese	35 m (about 40 yd)

The cartridge must also be compatible with the gun you are using; see proofing on page 31.

PLANNING
Always plan your wildfowling outings very carefully.

When you go on the foreshore for the first time, go in daylight with someone who knows the area and can point out marsh boundaries and any inherent dangers which occur.

When wildfowling away from home, it is courteous to make contact with the Secretaries of any local wildfowling clubs to ensure you do not inadvertently encroach on private ground.

Always tell someone where and when you are going wildfowling.

Do not forget to tell them you have returned safely.

Always make sure you know of local rules and restrictions.

You should be particularly aware of those rules that may be operating in a controlled shooting area. It is the sportsman's responsibility to find out about them before going onto a marsh.

Always consult Tide Tables before going on the marsh.

Always avoid the more distant parts of the marsh when a big tide is expected.
Remember that the figures stated will be altered by the prevailing weather conditions. Winds particularly can affect tide levels. Remember, if British Summer Time is in force, to make the necessary correction to your Tide Table.

EQUIPMENT
Always pay particular attention to equipment; check its condition before going wildfowling.

The following items of equipment are recommended:
Waterproof wristwatch – essential for judging the state of the tide;
Waterproof torch – but remember torch flashing is *only* justified in an emergency;
Binoculars – useful for identification purposes;

Six-foot wading pole – assists walking on the marsh, useful for sounding gutters and crossing places;

Pocket compass – essential in order to be able to work out direction to your chosen point and for establishing a safe return route, especially in mist or fog.

Pull-through – a means of cleaning barrels if snow or mud enters them. A piece of rag on a cord is adequate.

If you are going out all day, carry some food and a thermos containing a hot drink.

Make sure you take necessary documents with you:

Shotgun Certificate

Game Licence (if you intend to shoot Snipe or Woodcock)

Local Permit (if applicable).

Wear comfortable, inconspicuous, warm, waterproof clothing. Waders are normally recommended.

Always take a large canvas bag – it is often useful to sit on.

If you are using a punt or boat, make sure that it is seaworthy and that you have paddles/oars, anchor, baler, life-jacket and emergency flares.

A responsible shot will have Third Party Liability Insurance cover, but the best insurance is to follow the B.A.S.C. Shotgun Safety Code.

BEHAVIOUR ON THE MARSH

Always remember that the wildfowlers' main quarry – wild geese and ducks – are largely migrants and as such are an internationally shared resource; we have a responsibility to safeguard them and their environment.

Remember a marsh can be spoilt by continual human disturbance: you need not be shooting to cause a disturbance.

Always remember that others judge the sport of wildfowling by your behaviour.

One foolish or irresponsible act brings the whole sport into disrepute. Do not disturb the locality or other sportsmen by making a noise, banging car doors when arriving early in the morning or leaving late at night.

Never arrive late, or depart early, in relation to flight times (which will vary according to tides, winds, etc.); and do not disturb the shooting of those who have taken the trouble to get into position in good time.

Do not shoot in the immediate vicinity of houses adjoining the shore.

Make sure you are well hidden: camouflage yourself to suit your surroundings.

Look through your gun barrels to make sure they are clear whenever an obstruction may have entered.

Range-judging when wildfowling is particularly difficult as the flight develops; don't spoil it by shooting too early at out-of-range birds.

Take care to recognise legal quarry: if in doubt, don't shoot.

Never leave cartridge cases or unsightly pit-holes on the marsh.

Never try to be clever waiting for the last moment to leave the marsh when the incoming tide is approaching. Channels fill quickly and in a very short time they become a torrent.

Always condemn unsporting shooting i.e. at poor fliers and at birds out of range.

Always be accompanied by a gundog.

A dog is essential for tide shooting and picking-up after dark, but keep it under control at all times.
  Dogging the tideline will often recover lost birds.
  Try and make your dog comfortable; if you sit on your game bag, make sure that he has a dry seat.
  Send your dog to retrieve birds as they are shot. The tide may carry the birds away.

Always mark wounded quarry and ensure that it is picked up and humanely despatched as soon as possible.

A sharp knock on the head with a suitably heavy stick or priest is most effective.

ON LEAVING THE MARSH

Always consider the needs of your dog before your own.

He may be cold and wet: dry him and provide him with a dog blanket or bedding to lie on.

Always take care of your quarry.

Ensure that it is hung in a cool, dry place. Do not waste it.

Always pay special attention to cleaning your gun.

Mud and saltwater will quickly corrode it. Check it for faults which may need rectifying.

Whatever form of shooting you engage in, whether it be rough-shooting, formal driven game shooting or coastal wildfowling, your enjoyment of the sport will be increased by the presence of a well trained gundog. There are four very sound reasons why the B.A.S.C. strongly recommends that anyone who goes shooting should be accompanied by a trained and competent gundog. A dog can find, retrieve and bring to hand quarry which falls into thick cover or into or across water and which therefore could not be picked up by the shooter. A gundog is also able to find and retrieve game which is only wounded. A gundog is able to cover ground and search undergrowth which the shooter is not able to and thus increases the chances of finding and flushing quarry. Equally important is the fact that a dog is a wonderful companion and will make a shooting day more varied, interesting and enjoyable.

GUNDOGS

All breeds of gundogs have their supporters and good and bad examples of all the breeds can be seen in the shooting field. It does not really matter which breed of gundog you choose, but the following is an outline of the various breeds and the manner in which they are generally used.

RETRIEVERS

The primary function of Retrievers is to search for and retrieve dead or wounded quarry. Retrievers are frequently used by game shooters who stand at pegs or by pickers-up on formal driven game shoots. Due to the nature of the coat of the Labrador Retriever, it is a good dog for the wildfowler as it does not suffer from the cold to any great extent. Of the four Retriever breeds the black Labrador is the most common.

The breeds in this group are:

The Curly-coated Retriever

The Flatcoated Retriever

The Labrador Retriever

The Golden Retriever

SPANIELS

Spaniels are used primarily for questing – that is to hunt or search ground and cover in order to flush quarry. By far the most popular is the English Springer Spaniel which can be either liver and white, black and white or a tricolour combination of black, liver and white.

The breeds in this group are:

The English Springer Spaniel

The Welsh Springer Spaniel

The Cocker Spaniel

The Sussex Spaniel

The Field Spaniel

The Clumber Spaniel

The Irish Water Spaniel

POINTERS AND SETTERS The purpose of Pointers and Setters is to range in front of the gun or guns and to indicate the presence of quarry by adopting a rigid pose. This is called pointing.
The breeds in this group are:

The English Pointer　　　　　　*The English Setter*

The Gordon Setter　　　　　　*The Irish Setter*

ALL-PURPOSE GUNDOGS The purpose of these breeds is to hunt, point, flush and retrieve. The breeds in this group are:

The German Short-haired Pointer　　　*The Vizsla*

The Weimeraner　　　　　*The Large Munsterlander*

Having established the various breeds which are normally used for different purposes, it must be stressed that it is up to the individual to decide which breed is most suitable for his type of shooting and circumstances.

ACQUIRING A GUNDOG

If you consider your gun to be the most important piece of equipment, then certainly your dog comes a close second. You must therefore give great care and consideration to the acquisition of a gundog.

You may decide to buy a puppy, usually between 8 and 12 weeks old; or you may decide to buy a fully trained adult dog or a dog which is only partly trained. The choice is up to the individual and depends upon various circumstances. It is not our intention within this chapter to even begin to explain to you how to set about training a gundog, but simply to make you aware of a number of basic points which you should consider even before acquiring one. You must obviously give thought to kennelling, feeding, diet, cost and the dog's need for exercise. All gundogs need to be fit: they require a considerable amount of regular exercise.

BASIC TRAINING OF GUNDOGS

Should you decide to acquire a puppy, you will also have to decide whether or not you will train it yourself or whether you will send it away to be trained. If you decide to train the dog yourself, work out a programme or follow the guidelines as laid down in a recommended book, such as *Know Your Gundog Training* by Roy Jordan.

Briefly, basic training should consist of sitting to command, walking to heel, stopping immediately on command, stopping and sitting to shot, coming back when called, understanding the command 'No', observing directional hand signals, being steady to moving quarry and dropping to flush. Never take an untrained dog into the shooting field as it will spoil the enjoyment of all.

DOG HANDLING IN THE FIELD

When out shooting with your dog there is a certain code of conduct which you should follow at all times:

Always carry a lead and use it whenever you have to walk your dog along a road.

Always keep your dog under control at all times and do not allow it to disturb livestock.

Always check with your host that you can take your dog with you when invited out shooting.

If your host has organised pickers-up, your dog may not be welcome.

Always see to your dog's comfort before looking after yourself after a day's shooting.

If you have to travel, make sure that its bed in the car is warm. When you get home, check it for thorns and cuts and give any treatment necessary.

Always rub your dog down with a sack or towel if it is wet after a day's shooting.

See that its kennel is dry and draughtproof with a comfortable bed.

Never allow your dog to pick up quarry shot by another shooter except with his agreement.

This is important as shooters must keep a count of how many birds they have down at any one time in order to make sure that every bird which is shot is retrieved.

A shooter may also wish his own dog to retrieve a bird which he has shot.

Never allow your dog to take dead or wounded quarry from another dog.

Never allow your dog to fight with other dogs or to worry bitches.

Never take a bitch which is in season into the company of other dogs in the field.

Never have a collar on your dog when it is working.

Dogs have been hung by collars when going over banks, down gullies and over walls. Dogs have also been drowned when a branch or wire under water has caught on a collar.

Never attach your dog's lead to yourself when shooting.

Never send your dog over the boundary of your shoot unless you have permission to do so.

Never overtire your dog.

If your dog has had a very hard morning, it is much better to leave it in the car after lunch or make it walk to heel in the afternoon, rather than overtire it.

A keen and alert pupil sits on command.

Following directional hand signals.

Steadiness in company is essential.

Training should be enjoyable – for man and dog.

Gamekeeping

Anyone who actually takes part in game shooting and/or rough-shooting should understand the work of a gamekeeper, and appreciate his role in habitat and game management.

THE ROLE OF THE GAMEKEEPER

A gamekeeper is employed on a shoot to look after and encourage the game population. He does this by either protecting the wild stock, and thus allowing them to breed, or by rearing and releasing game birds thus augmenting the overall game population.

IN HABITAT CREATION
AND MANAGEMENT

It is necessary to create a suitable environment for a healthy game population. The gamekeeper achieves this by planting hedges, spinneys and game crops on the shoot. These provide food, nesting cover and shelter for game birds and thus the 'carrying capacity' of the shoot is increased.

IN CONSERVATION

A keepered environment sustains a greater overall wildlife population than an unkeepered environment. The reason for this is that the gamekeeper, whilst looking after the interests of the game population by creating or protecting existing habitat and killing vermin which predate upon game, is providing habitat and protected surroundings for songbirds, wild animals and plants. In this way he is making a valuable contribution to the conservation of the countryside.

THE NEED TO
SUPPLEMENT WILD
GAMEBIRD STOCKS

Wild gamebird populations may need to be supplemented by rearing and releasing additional stocks. On a shoot where there are not large stocks of gamebirds (Pheasants, Grey and Red-legged Partridges) and duck to provide sport for the guns, then it is the gamekeeper's job to rear and release game to supplement the wild population.

MEANS OF INCREASING
THE STOCK OF
GAMEBIRDS

There are four main ways of doing this:

*1 Releasing from egg
production to poult*

Game birds are caught and penned before the end of the shooting season (December–January). The following spring these captive birds produce eggs which are incubated either artificially in incubators or under broody hens. The resulting chicks are reared by the gamekeeper and released into the wild at 6–8 weeks old. The release programme is a gradual process, thus allowing the young gamebirds to acclimatise to their new surroundings.

2 Releasing from purchased eggs to poult stage

Eggs are bought from a reputable game farm which sells large numbers of gamebird eggs, chicks and poults (young gamebirds). These eggs are incubated; the chicks are reared by the gamekeeper and then released on to the shoot at 6–8 weeks old

3 Releasing from purchased chick to poult stage

Day-old gamebird chicks are bought from a game farm, the chicks are reared and released onto the shoot by the gamekeeper.

4 Releasing bought in poults

6–8 week old poults are purchased from a game farm and released gradually onto the shoot.

VERMIN CONTROL

The control of both ground and avian vermin is of utmost importance if gamebirds are to thrive on a shoot. If the vermin population is not kept in check, then nesting gamebirds and recently released poults would have little chance of survival. So it is the gamekeeper's job to control vermin.

Vermin can be defined as animals which predate upon eggs, chicks, poults and adult gamebirds, and can be divided into two categories:

1 Ground Predators:

These are animals which predate at times upon game and live and breed at ground level. These include: Fox, Feral Cat, Mink, Stoat, Weasel, Polecat, Brown Rat and Hedgehog.

2 Avian Predators:

These are birds which often predate upon gamebird eggs and chicks and include: Carrion Crow, Hooded Crow, Rook, Jackdaw, Magpie, Jay, Greater Black-backed Gull and Lesser Black-backed Gull.

There are other avian predators which are protected by the Wildlife and Countryside Act 1981 (see page 138) and should not be killed.

METHODS OF VERMIN CONTROL

There are five main methods of vermin control that are available to a gamekeeper:

1 Shooting

The gamekeeper usually carries a shotgun with him when he is working on the shoot and often has the chance to shoot both ground and avian predators.

2 Trapping – Tunnel Traps

Artificial tunnels are placed at strategic points round the estate. A Fenn Mk IV Spring Trap is placed, and set, in each of these tunnels. Ground vermin (except foxes and feral cats) hunting for food will investigate these tunnels and be caught in the trap.

3 Trapping – Cage Traps

Cage traps of different varieties will catch all avian and ground predators. They have either to be baited with food, or camouflaged to look like a natural tunnel, to entice the vermin to enter.

4 Snaring	The use of free-running snares, set correctly according to the B.A.S.C. Snaring Code of Practice, is the most efficient way of controlling the number of foxes on a shoot.
5 Poison	The correct use of legally prescribed poison (e.g. Warfarin) is a very efficient way of controlling certain vermin, such as a rat infestation on a shoot.
SHOOT DAY MANAGEMENT	It is the gamekeeper's responsibility to ensure that everything runs smoothly on a shoot day. He is responsible for organising the following:
1 Guns	He makes sure that numbered pegs are correctly positioned at each drive (see Chapter 8: Game Shooting).
2 Beaters	He organises the line of beaters on the day.
3 Pickers-up	He ensures that there are people with well trained dogs at each drive, behind the line of guns, to humanely retrieve shot and wounded game.
4 Stops	He makes sure that these are strategically and correctly sited at each drive.
5 Storage and sale of Game	The gamekeeper must ensure that the shot game is handled and stored correctly, thus guaranteeing that, when it is sold to the game-dealer, it commands a realistic price.
POACHING AND TRESPASS	Disturbance of game must be kept to a minimum. It is important that game is not subjected to a lot of human disturbance, and it is the gamekeeper's job to ensure that this is kept to an absolute minimum.

Appendix 1

OFFICIALLY DESIGNATED AREAS OF LANDSCAPE OR CONSERVATION VALUE

SITES OF SPECIAL SCIENTIFIC INTEREST (S.S.S.I.s)

Over the past thirty years the Nature Conservancy Council (N.C.C.), the official body responsible for nature conservation, has identified areas of special scientific interest throughout Great Britain that are judged to be of special importance for their wildlife or geological or physiographical features.

The prime purpose of S.S.S.I.s is to provide an objective list of areas which need to be monitored and protected. Some of these areas are nature reserves but many are not. S.S.S.I.s are subject to a certain amount of legislative protection governing their management by owners and occupiers. Shooting men considering management schemes on S.S.S.I.s should seek advice from the B.A.S.C. during the planning stages.

NATIONAL NATURE RESERVES (N.N.R.)

National nature reserves protect some of the country's best wildlife habitats and are managed by the Nature Conservancy Council. Caerlaverock N.N.R., Lindisfarne N.N.R., and the Bridgewater Bay N.N.R. are examples.

LOCAL NATURE RESERVES (L.N.R.)

These fall under the responsibility of a local authority in consultation with the Nature Conservancy Council. Management may be designated to voluntary conservation bodies.

OTHER DESIGNATED AREAS

These include areas such as national parks, areas of outstanding natural beauty and green belts which may be set aside for their landscape features and which provide for recreation or amenity. In order to protect these valuable sites certain planning controls are applied by appropriate local authorities.

AREAS OF SPECIAL PROTECTION FOR BIRDS

These areas are set up by the minister for the environment to provide special protection for birds where it is necessary. In earlier legislation they were called Sanctuaries.

Appendix 2

CONSERVATION RESEARCH STUDIES
CONDUCTED BY THE B.A.S.C.

NATIONAL SHOOTING
PROGRAMME

This programme provides information on the numbers and distribution of the wild quarry birds shot each year. By keeping a shooting register and contributing to such survey work as requested, the shooting man can help the B.A.S.C. in producing an accurate and factual account of sporting shooting in Britain, essential to the long-term management of the quarry species and shooting.

DUCK WING SURVEY

By sending one wing from each duck that he shoots to the B.A.S.C., the sportsman helps to reveal the age, sex and species composition of the wintering duck populations, as well as different migratory patterns.

This information is invaluable for the management of wildfowl stocks in relation to shooting.

WOODCOCK PRODUCTION
SURVEY

A similar scheme of wing collections is conducted for woodcock. One wing from each bird shot should be sent to the B.A.S.C. to help monitor this elusive bird's breeding success and movements.

RINGING STUDIES

Any ring or other mark found or seen on a bird should be reported as directed on the ring, or to the B.A.S.C., since recoveries of marked birds are vital to the success of many wildfowl studies.

Appendix 3

PROOF MARKS

BRITISH PROOF MARKS

Because the introduction of new proof regulations and markings does not of itself render invalid earlier proof marks, guns may validly bear proof marks impressed under Rules of Proof of 1954, 1925 or even earlier. The majority of shotguns in use at the present time (Jan 1976) have been proved or reproved since 1925. Marks are normally impressed on the flats of shotgun barrels or otherwise near the breech and upon the action.

UNDER 1954 RULES OF PROOF

The proof marks at present (1976) impressed by the London and Birmingham Proof Houses are as follows:

		London	Birmingham
1 Provisional proof			
3 Definitive proof for nitro powders	on action		BNP
	on barrel	NP	BNP
4 Definitive proof for Black Powder only			BP
	and the words	NOT NITRO	BLACK POWDER
6 Special definitive proof			SP

	London	Birmingham
7 Reproof	👑 ℛ	👑 R

Additionally arms will bear markings to indicate the maximum mean pressure* of cartridges for which the arm has been proved together with the nominal gauge (in a diamond, as ⬦) and chamber length or nominal calibre and case length. Shotguns will also bear marks to indicate the nominal bore diameter, as found at 9 in. from the breech, shown in decimals e.g. .729 in.

UNDER 1925 RULES OF PROOF

The Provisional, Special Proof and Reproof marks were similar to marks 1, 6 and 7, but the following different markings should be noted.

		London	Birmingham
Definitive	Proof	👑 GP	👑 BP
	View	👑 V	👑 BV
	Nitro	NP	👑 NP

together with the words NITRO PROOF

Military proof		🦁 NP	👑 BM

N.B.   The encirclement of marks impressed under these Rules

* *In exceptional cases maximum service loads may be marked in lieu of service pressures.*

as accompanied by the words Not English Make indicated proof of a foreign arm.

Additionally marks were used to indicate nominal bore diameter (such as 12 or $\frac{13}{1}$), nominal gauge (in a diamond, as ⬦), chamber length and maximum shot load. In the case of rifles, marks will indicate the nominal calibre and case length and the maximum service load of powder and bullet.

UNDER RULES OF PROOF PRIOR TO 1904

The following Definitive proof marks were in use at the Birmingham Proof House from 1813 until August 1904.

Birmingham Company Proof   View

These marks invariably indicate proof for Black Powder unless they are associated with the marking Nitro Proof in words.

Between 1887 and 1925 the following marks were used to denote special Definitive proof of barrels proved once only. They may appear on single-barrel shotguns and on certain rifled arms.

	London	Birmingham

CONCLUSION

Advice as to the interpretation of the marks which cannot be identified from these notes should be sought from either Proof House.

Advice as to complaints
The Proof Houses were established for public safety and are in being to ensure, by means of rigorous proof tests on every individual barrel and chamber, sound standards of materials and manufacture for all types of firearms and thus a greater measure of safety for those handling them.

To this end one of the more important functions of the Proof Authorities is to ensure observance of the regulations and to institute proceedings against offenders where the necessary evidence is put before them and is considered to justify such action.

Closer co-operation between the shooting public, gunmakers

and the Proof Authorities must result in a reduction of the risks involved in buying secondhand and foreign arms, whether through chance acquaintance, unscrupulous dealers or misinformed friends.

Information as to offences and all enquiries on proof matters should be addressed as below. The Proof Masters will gladly give all possible assistance and advice.

The Proof Master
The Proof House, 48 Commercial Road, London E1

The Proof Master
The Gun Barrel Proof House, Banbury Street, Birmingham B5 5RH

SPANISH PROOF MARKS
Proof House at Eibar

No.	Mark	Type of proof	Type of arm	Location of marks
1		Arms proved at Eibar	All	Action or frame or body
2		Definitive Black Powder	Muzzle loading smooth bore guns	Barrel and breech closure
3		Provisional Black Powder	Tubes of breech loading shotguns	Barrel
4		Definitive Black Powder	Breech loading shotguns	Barrel and action or body
5		Definitive	Long barrelled rifled arms	Barrel, frame and bolt
6		Definitive	Saloon pistols and small bore guns	Barrel, frame or body, bolt or slide
7		Definitive Black Powder	Non automatic pistols	Barrel, breech closure and body
8		Definitive	Revolvers	Barrel, cylinder and body
9		Definitive	Auto pistols	Barrel, slide and body
10		Arms made to a standard	All parts	Action or frame or body according to the type of arm

No.	Mark	Type of proof	Type of arm	Location of marks
11	BP	Obligatory nitro proof	All breech loading shotguns	Barrel and action or frame
12	CH	Supplementary or magnum nitro proof	Breech loading shotguns	Barrel and action or frame
13	E	Definitive	All foreign arms	Corresponding position to 2, 5, 6, 7, 8, 9, 11 and 12 according to the type of arm

There are other marks used, as for instance to indicate gauge, bore diameter and chamber length in millimetres, but they are in addition to those described above.

Note: Earlier proof marks not shown here may still be valid. The Proof Masters will advise in cases of doubt.

Appendix 4

WILDLIFE AND COUNTRYSIDE ACT 1981

SCHEDULE 1
Birds which are protected by Special Penalties

Part 1
AT ALL TIMES

Common name	Scientific name	Common name	Scientific name
Avocet	Recurvirostra avosetta	Kite, Red	Milvus milvus
Bee-eater	Merops apiaster	Merlin	Falco columbarius
Bittern	Botaurus stellaris	Oriole, Golden	Oriolus oriolus
Bittern, Little	Ixobrychus minutus	Osprey	Pandion haliaetus
Bluethroat	Luscinia svecica	Owl, Barn	Tyto alba
Brambling	Fringilla monti-fringilla	Owl, Snowy	Nyctea scandiaca
		Peregrine	Falco peregrinus
Bunting, Cirl	Emberiza cirlus	Petrel, Leach's	Oceanodroma leucorhoa
Bunting, Lapland	Calcarius lapponicus		
Bunting, Snow	Plectrophenax nivalis	Phalarope, Red-necked	Phalaropus lobatus
Buzzard, Honey	Pernis apivorus		
Chough	Pyrrhocorax pyrrhocorax	Plover, Kentish	Charadrius alexandrinus
Corncrake	Crex crex	Plover, Little Ringed	Charadrius dubius
Crake, Spotted	Porzana porzana	Quail, Common	Coturnix coturnix
Crossbills (all species)	Loxia spp.	Redstart, Black	Phoenicurus ochruros
Curlew, Stone	Burhinus oedicnemus	Redwing	Turdus iliacus
Divers (all species)	Gavia spp.	Rosefinch, Scarlet	Carpodacus erythrinus
Dotterel	Charadrius morinellus	Ruff	Philomachus pugnax
Duck, Long-tailed	Clangula hyemalis	Sandpiper, Green	Tringa ochropus
Eagle, Golden	Aquila chrysaetos	Sandpiper, Purple	Calidris maritima
Eagle, White-tailed	Haliaeetus albicilla	Sandpiper, Wood	Tringa glareola
Falcon, Gyr	Falco rusticolus	Scaup	Aythya marila
Fieldfare	Turdus pilaris	Scoter, Common	Melanitta nigra
Firecrest	Regulus ignicapillus	Scoter, Velvet	Melanitta fusca
Garganey	Anas querquedula	Serin	Serinus serinus
Godwit, Black-tailed	Limosa limosa	Shorelark	Eremophila alpestris
Goshawk	Accipiter gentilis	Shrike, Red-backed	Lanius collurio
Grebe, Black-necked	Podiceps nigricollis	Spoonbill	Platalea leucorodia
Grebe, Slavonian	Podiceps auritus	Stilt, Black-winged	Himantopus himantopus
Greenshank	Tringa nebularia		
Gull, Little	Larus minutus	Stint, Temminck's	Calidris temminckii
Gull, Mediterranean	Larus melanocephalus	Swan, Beswick's	Cygnus bewickii
		Swan, Whooper	Cygnus cygnus
Harriers (all species)	Circus spp.	Tern, Black	Chlidonias niger
Heron, Purple	Ardea purpurea	Tern, Little	Sterna albifrons
Hobby	Falco subbuteo	Tern, Roseate	Sterna dougallii
Hoopoe	Upupa epops	Tit, Bearded	Panurus biarmicus
Kingfisher	Alcedo atthis	Tit, Crested	Parus cristatus

Common name	Scientific name	Common name	Scientific name
Treecreeper, Short-toed	Certhia brachydactyla	Warbler, Savi's	Locustella luscinioides
Warbler, Cetti's	Cettia cetti	Whimbrel	Numenius phaeopus
Warbler, Dartford	Sylvia undata	Woodlark	Lullula arborea
Warbler, Marsh	Acrocephalus palustris	Wryneck	Jynx torquilla

Part II
DURING THE CLOSE SEASON

Common name	Scientific name
Goldeneye	Bucephala clangula
Goose, Greylag (in Outer Hebrides, Caithness, Sutherland and Wester Ross only)	Anser anser
Pintail	Anas acuta

Note: The common name or names given in the first column of this Schedule are included by way of guidance only; in the event of any dispute or proceedings, the common name or names shall not be taken into account.

SCHEDULE 2
Birds Which May be Killed or Taken

Part I
OUTSIDE THE CLOSE SEASON

Common name	Scientific name	Common name	Scientific name
Capercaillie	Tetrao urogallus	Mallard	Anas platyrhynchos
Coot	Fulica atra	Moorhen	Gallinula chloropus
Duck, Tufted	Aythya fuligula	Pintail	Anas acuta
Gadwall	Anas strepera	Plover, Golden	Pluvialis apricaria
Goldeneye	Bucephala clangula	Pochard	Aythya ferina
Goose, Canada	Branta canadensis	Shoveler	Anas clypeata
Goose, Greylag	Anser anser	Snipe, Common	Gallinago gallinago
Goose, Pink-footed	Anser brachyrhynchus	Teal	Anas crecca
		Wigeon	Anas penelope
Goose, White-fronted (in England and Wales only)	Anser albifrons	Woodcock	Scolopax rusticola

Part II
BY AUTHORISED PERSONS AT ALL TIMES

Common name	Scientific name	Common name	Scientific name
Crow	Corvus corone	Rook	Corvus frugilegus
Dove, Collared	Streptopelia decaocto	Sparrow, House	Passer domesticus
Gull, Great Black-backed	Larus marinus	Starling	Sturnus vulgaris
		Woodpigeon	Columba palumbus
Gull, Lesser Black-backed	Larus fuscus		
Gull, Herring	Larus argentatus		
Jackdaw	Corvus monedula		
Jay	Garrulus glandarius		
Magpie	Pica pica		
Pigeon, Feral	Columba livia		

Note: The common name or names given in the first column of this Schedule are included by way of guidance only; in the event of any dispute or proceedings, the common name or names shall not be taken into account.

SCHEDULE 3
Birds Which May be Sold

Part I
ALIVE AT ALL TIMES IF RINGED AND BRED IN CAPTIVITY

Common name	Scientific name	Common name	Scientific name
Blackbird	Turdus merula	Jay	Garrulus glandarius
Brambling	Fringilla monti-fringilla	Linnet	Carduelis cannabina
		Magpie	Pica pica
Bullfinch	Pyrrhula pyrrhula	Owl, Barn	Tyto alba
Bunting, Reed	Emberiza schoeniclus	Redpoll	Carduelis flammea
Chaffinch	Fringilla coelebs	Siskin	Carduelis spinus
Dunnock	Prunella modularis	Starling	Sturnus vulgaris
Goldfinch	Carduelis carduelis	Thrush, Song	Turdus philomelos
Greenfinch	Carduelis chloris	Twite	Carduelis flavirostris
Jackdaw	Corvus monedula	Yellowhammer	Emberiza citrinella

Part II
DEAD AT ALL TIMES

Common name	Scientific name	Common name	Scientific name
Pigeon, Feral	Columba livia	Woodpigeon	Columba palumbus

Part III
DEAD FROM 1 SEPTEMBER TO 28 FEBRUARY

Common name	Scientific name	Common name	Scientific name
Capercaillie	Tetrao urogallus	Pochard	Aythya ferina
Coot	Fulica atra	Shoveler	Anas clypeata
Duck, Tufted	Aythya fuligula	Snipe, Common	Gallinago gallinago
Mallard	Anas platyrhynchos	Teal	Anas crecca
Pintail	Anas acuta	Wigeon	Anas penelope
Plover, Golden	Pluvialis apricaria	Woodcock	Scolopax rusticola

Note: The common name or names given in the first column of this Schedule are included by way of guidance only; in the event of any dispute or proceedings, the common name or names shall not be taken into account.

SCHEDULE 5
Animals which are Protected

Adder	Butterfly, Large Blue	Lizard, Sand	Otter, Common
Bats, Horseshoe (all species)	Butterfly, Swallowtail	Lizard, Viviparous	Porpoise, Harbour
Bats, Typical (all species)	Cricket, Field	Moth, Barberry Carpet	Slow-worm
Beetle, Rainbow Leaf	Cricket, Mole	Moth, Black-veined	Snail, Carthusian
Burbot	Dolphin, Bottle-nosed	Moth, Essex Emerald	Snail, Glutinous
Butterfly, Chequered Skipper	Dolphin, Common	Moth, New Forest Burnet	Snail, Sandbowl
Butterfly, Heath Fritillary	Dragonfly, Norfolk Aeshna	Moth, Reddish Buff	Snake, Grass
	Frog, Common	Newt, Great Crested	Snake, Smooth
	Grasshopper, Wart-biter	Newt, Palmate	Spider, Fen Raft
		Newt, Smooth	Spider, Ladybird
			Squirrel, Red
			Toad, Common
			Toad, Natterjack

Appendix 5

SHOOTING A MOVING TARGET

There are several recognised methods of consistently shooting a moving target. The method outlined below is that used by the Clay Pigeon Shooting Association to coach beginners.

The C.P.S.A. approved method is based on three principles:

1 When the gun is properly mounted (raised into the shoulder), it should point in the direction in which the shooter is looking.

2 The easiest thing to look at is the target.

3 In all forms of shotgun shooting, at the moment of firing, the barrels are aligned so as to place the shot in front of the target along its line of flight. This is generally referred to as 'lead'.

The secret of successful shooting is to use these three fundamental principles to produce the correct effect.

To develop these basic points further:

1 Make sure that you are shooting from the correct shoulder and that your 'master eye' is placed directly over the line of the barrel(s); how to test for 'master eye' is explained on page 23. Gunfit is obviously also important in order to ensure that the 'master eye' is correctly aligned over the barrels. You must practise mounting the gun into the shoulder.

2 Practise looking at moving targets and pointing at them, either with a finger or with a shotgun (always empty – safety first).

3 The exact amount of 'lead' required for each moving target can only be learned by actual experience of shooting. Each individual sportsman develops his own 'picture' of bird-gunbarrel alignment at the moment of firing.

The method can be illustrated diagrammatically:

| GUN READY | SEE TARGET AND MOUNT | MAINTAIN CONTACT | MOVE IN FRONT AND FIRE | FOLLOW THROUGH | GUN DOWN AND OPEN |

As the shooter sees the bird, he will try and keep the tip of the barrels on the target as he mounts the gun. When the gunstock meets the cheek, there should be a straight line between the eye and the bird, with the barrel tip lying along that line. In swinging with the bird, the swinging action from the feet, to the hips and waist, will keep the alignment going.

Keep the swing going for a moment to establish the speed of the bird, pointing at the bird all the time, then 'move in front', fire and follow through. (Remember that the amount of 'lead' will vary depending upon the speed and range of the target.)

This sequence of diagrams is for a left-to-right crossing bird. If the bird is a right-to-left crosser, the sequence is naturally reversed.

It is important to remember the following points:

(*i*) the swing and the mount occur simultaneously;

(*ii*) there is a short period of time when the gun is pointing directly at the bird;

(*iii*) the correct 'barrel-target' picture is essential to consistent successful shooting;

(*iv*) the 'follow through' is essential in order to overcome the tendency to stop the swing of the gun on firing.

Index